ON YOUR KNEES

Biblical references, Religion and

Faith in the songs by U2

BARBARA MARINELLO

Titolo | On your Knees
Autore | Barbara Marinello
ISBN | 978-88-93329-48-4

Youcanprint Self-Publishing
Via Roma, 73 - 73039 Tricase (LE) - Italy
www.youcanprint.it
info@youcanprint.it
Facebook: facebook.com/youcanprint.it
Twitter: twitter.com/youcanprintit

To all those who have been able to understand and encourage me.
To all those who have been, are or will be part of my life.
To Paul David Hewson, my light through the darkness.
God bless U2

INDEX

INTRODUCTION...pg 1

CHAPTER I..pg 7
The band...pg 9

CHAPTER II..pg 15
Boy..pg 17
I will follow ....pg 19
Twilight ....pg 20
Into the heart ....pg 21
Out of control..pg 21
Another time another place...pg 22

CHAPTER III...pg 23
October ....pg 25
Gloria...pg 26
I threw a brick through a window..pg 27
Rejoice ....pg 27
Fire ....pg 28
Tomorrow ....pg 29
October ....pg 29
With a shout...pg 30
Scarlet ....pg 31
Stranger in a strange land..pg 31

CHAPTER IV...pg 33
War ....pg 35
Sunday bloody Sunday.. pg 36
Seconds...pg 37
New Year's Day.. pg 38
Like a song...pg 38
Drowning Man.. pg 40
Two hearts beat as one.. pg 41
Red light..pg 41
Surrender ....pg 42
40 ....pg 43

CHAPTER V...pg 47
The unforgettable fire..pg 49
A sort of homecoming..pg 50
Pride...pg 51
Wire ....pg 53
The unforgettable fire...pg 54
Promenade..pg 54
Indian summer sky...pg 55
Elvis Presley and America.....................................pg 56

CHAPTER VI...pg 59
The Joshua tree..pg 61
Where the streets have no name.............................pg 62
I still haven't found what I'm looking for.................pg 64
With or without you..pg 65
Bullet the blue sky..pg 68
Running to stand still..pg 69
Red hill mining town...pg 71
In God's country..pg 72
Trip through your wires...pg 74
One tree hill..pg 74
Exit..pg 75

CHAPTER VII..pg 77
Rattle and hum...pg 79
Helter skelter...pg 80
Desire...pg 81
Hawkmoon 269..pg 82
All along the watchtower..pg 84
I still haven't found what I'm looking for.................pg 86
Silver and gold..pg 86
Love rescue me..pg 88
When love comes to town......................................pg 90
God part II..pg 91
All I want is you..pg 93

CHAPTER VIII...pg 95

Achtung baby..pg 97

Zoostation..pg 99

Even better than the real thing...pg 99

One...pg 100

Until the end of the world..pg 103

Who's gonna ride your wild horses...pg 106

So cruel..pg 107

The fly...pg 110

Mysterious ways...pg 112

Tryin' to throw your arms around the world..................................pg 114

Ultraviolet (light my way)..pg 114

Acrobat...pg 115

Love is blindness...pg 116

CHAPTER IX...pg 119

Zooropa...pg 121

Lemon...pg 122

Stay (faraway so close)..pg 124

Daddy's gonna pay for your crashed car......................................pg 126

Some days are better than others..pg 127

The first time...pg 128

The wanderer..pg 130

The character of Macphisto: meaning and symbology...........................pg 134

CHAPTER X...pg 137

Pop...pg 139

Discoheque..pg 140

Do you feel loved...pg 141

Mofo..pg 142

If God will send His Angels..pg 144

Staring at the sun..pg 145

Last night on earth...pg 146

The playboy mansion...pg 148

If you wear that velvet dress...pg 150

Please..pg 151

Wake up dead man..pg 153

CHAPTER XI..pg 157

All that you can't leave behind...............................pg 159

Beautiful day...pg 161

Stuck in a moment you can't get out of........................pg 162

Elevation...pg 164

Walk on...pg 165

Kite..pg 167

In a little while...pg 169

Wild honey..pg 170

Peace on earth..pg 172

When I look at the world......................................pg 173

New York..pg 175

Grace...pg 175

The ground beneath her feet...................................pg 178

CHAPTER XII...pg 181

How to dismantle an atomic bomb...............................pg 183

Vertigo...pg 184

Miracle drug..pg 187

Sometimes you can't make it on your own.......................pg 190

Love and peace or else..pg 191

City of blinding lights.......................................pg 193

All because of you..pg 196

A man and a woman...pg 198

Crumbs from your table..pg 200

One step closer...pg 202

Original of the species.......................................pg 203

Yahweh..pg 205

Fast cars...pg 207

CHAPTER XIII..pg 209

18 singles..pg 211

The saints are coming...pg 211

Windows in the sky..pg 213

CHAPTER XIV...pg 217

No line on the horizon..pg 219

No line on the horizon..pg 220

Magnificent..pg 221
Moment of surrender..pg 224
Unknown caller...pg 227
I'll go crazy if I don't go crazy tonight..................pg 229
Get on your boots..pg 230
Stand up comedy...pg 231
White as snow..pg 234
Breathe..pg 236
Cedars of Lebanon..pg 237

CHAPTER XV..pg 239
Bsides and miscellaneous tracks...........................pg 241
A celebration...pg 241
Alex descends into Hell for a bottle of Milk/ Korova 1........pg 243
Salomé...pg 243
Falling at your feet..pg 244
Always...pg 245
Levitate..pg 246
Mercy..pg 247
Waves of sorrow (Birdland)..................................pg 249
Hold me, thrill me, kiss me, kill me......................pg 251
Electrical storm...pg 253

CHAPTER XVI...pg 255
Conclusion...pg 257
Bibliography..pg 259

Introduction

INTRODUCTION

It's easy to talk about U2 considering their long career, their commitment in the world and all that has already been said and written about them.

The great variety of songs and the great variety of themes found in them means that there can not be an unambiguous interpretation of the message U2 want to convey with their music, but every single text can be perceived and analysed according to many guidelines, which vary according to what each one wants to read in every song, based on the historical moment in which we live, according to the society and culture from which we come, according to our inner being. So from politics to social issues, love, eroticism, the emotional and the spiritual merge and everything can be found in the same song. It just depends on what we want to read in it. But in the end is not this the sense of music? At least the real music that is played with the heart rather than with the instruments and the voice, now becomes only a means to convey emotions. If even just one of the messages that they want to be taken from a song touches us, it means that the goal has been reached.

In this book I want to take into consideration the religiosity of U2, from the group and the individual members of the group to an analysis song by song, from the origins up to today, of the biblical references that can be traced and a strictly religious interpretation of their lyrics. Of course this is a topic already covered by others, but this is such an important subject for the group and for those who have always followed it that there is always something more to say or add.

How important is religion to the training of the band is evidenced by the words of Bono himself: he says that the scriptures attract him because in him there is a dark side, and the Bible holds him up. He feels like a person who needs an anchor and firm reference points and the Bible, not seen as an historical book, provides him them and speaks to him leaving him a message that changes him from within.

There is a force of love and logic in the world, a force that guides the universe. This concept will be a common thread throughout the artistic and human history of U2. Faith leads on high, but it is spirituality rather than religion: religion often appears as an enemy of God, it is like a shell that encloses and often distorts its contents, which is the spirit that raises and conveys his message of love.

Heaven and Hell, the choice between good and evil, are always offered us and both are in us. Every U2 song contains this dichotomy and can be interpreted as earthly or spiritual, where earthly and spiritual merge into a single melody that conveys its message. Bono himself says: "the music that tells me something or leads to God or against God. In both cases, we recognize that God is the centre of the universe".

One of the recurring themes in the lyrics of U2 is religion and in particular the relationship with God. They used to say that the rock was the music of the devil, but Bono writes about religion, particularly taking inspiration from the Psalms. To define their music "rock of God" as opposed to the common idea of rock is perhaps exaggerated, but in November 1999, while rewarding U2 at the MTV Europe Awards in Dublin, Mick Jagger said: "This is the devil that rewards God".

The intent of this book is to try to analyse on the one hand the religious references that were clearly inserted by the band and their meaning, on the other hand the interpretation and meaning that fans can give depending on what they read or want to read.

Chapter 1

THE BAND

It was in Mount Temple Comprehensive High School in Dublin that the components of future U2 met. It was 1976 when Larry Mullen Junior put the announcement on the bulletin board looking for people to form a band. Answers came by Paul David Hewson (which actually was intended as a guitarist and was then taken as a singer), Adam Clayton, and Dave Evans who showed up with his brother Dick. Thus was born a group of guys with the name 'Feedback', just to give the idea that their intention was to do covers of other singers.

Shortly after the group changed its name into 'The Hype' and Dick left, thus arriving at the final formation. Maintaining that they were scarce musicians and definitely not good at playing the songs of others, they decided to start to write their own songs and so U2 were born. They took the name in March 1978 getting inspired either by the American spy plane that controlled the Soviet Union and was shot down in 1960 or by the subway line in Berlin, the most famous and with the most important historical references. They liked the name also because of the latent ambiguity in meaning. In 1978 the first recognition already came by winning a contest of rock music in Ireland and only a couple of years later they released their first album, Boy.

It was during a tour in the United States, where they tried to promote their music, that in 1982 they met the photographer Corbijn with which they settled a future collaboration to cure all the album covers and even videos.

In 1985 in Milan are the first dates of their Italian tour.

In more than 30 years that have passed since the beginning of their adventure U2 have made a musical evolution but managed to retain the same basic themes of their songs: politics, social engagement, the fight for peace and equal rights, love, feelings and emotions, religion and faith.

It was for religious reasons that, just starting out, the band even threatened to disband. In 1981 The Edge, Larry and Bono came to be part of a religious group called Shalom. Edge was so taken that he decided to leave the band. He returned some time later. Adam was the only one not to be touched and, just for being a non-believer, was often isolated from the group. The strong religiosity and spirituality already present from the earliest times never left the band but it was often an inspiration for the lyrics, especially the psalms and the Bible, which became the main text for the group.

Bono, whose real name is Paul David Hewson, was born in Dublin on May 10th, 1960 by a Protestant mother and a Catholic father. Considering how experienced on himself Bono was perhaps the most motivated to make deep reference to all that was Faith and spirituality and to bring these themes into his work and to all those who wanted to share them. At 14 he lost his mother and this event changed his life and his way of being. As a child he was so lively that he earned the nickname of "The Antichrist" but from here on there is a total approach to Christ and to God through Him.

Although normally in marriages between Catholics and Protestants the children were brought up in the principles of Catholicism, Bono attended elementary school at Inkwell, a school of the Protestant church. Thus he experiences the possibility of a peaceful encounter between different views: every Sunday his father accompanied his wife and children to function in the Church of Ireland and then take them back after witnessing the mass.

Later on even the death of his father Bob will impact on his vision and interpretation of religion, and songs will be obviously dedicated to his father. They can however easily be seen as songs to God, in the sense that the subject becomes the single person who realizes that he can not be and can not do anything without God, who is now the Father, the support, the reference.

The choice to follow the Catholic faith has so much influence in the text of many of the songs by U2. From the Book of Psalms (for which he also wrote an introduction) come numerous citations and references to God and the Bible can be found even in the more recent songs.

Bono himself explains his attachment to the Old Testament and his deep consideration of King David, the author of the Psalms, considered almost a "star" of the Bible. In an interview with L'Osservatore Romano Bono says: "At twelve I loved David, for me it was like a pop star, the words of the psalms were poetry and he was a star".

"Explaining faith has always been difficult. How can you explain love and logic in the heart when the world is so full of troubles? Explaining faith is impossible... it's vision more than visibility... it's instinct more than intellect "are Bono's words.

We have to underline the attachment to the Psalms that Bono always considers open for his inspiration and guidance. In the reading and study of the sacred texts, he begins to break away from religion, feeling increasingly pushed to the faith (Bono himself underlined the discrepancy between the two, with religion as a "perversion" of faith); he sees God in all things and with his music wants to convey this concept, thus making his religiosity not a fiction, not a mystical thing but "legendary", addressed to God.

The religious references that we find in some songs do not have the same meaning: as in a long inner journey also the message that is taken from their albums and their songs will change with the evolution of the group and with their interpersonal relationships, it changes with their personal experiences, with the changing times and needs of the public. So we can find at the beginning a deep and praised religiosity in songs that are prayers and hymns; we find then almost a detachment and loss of the religiosity expressed earlier that seems to fade to give way to the new gods of consumerism and money

But God is not dead. His image remains latent only to reappear renovated later in the last few albums. We no longer speak of religion but we find now spirituality, something superior that invades the entire universe. Along their journey we find the trinity: at first the praise of God, then the invocation of Christ, when it seems that God is no longer there, finally the renewed joy in the Holy Spirit who is pure love and leads to rebirth and harmony.

Chapter 2

BOY (Island 1979)

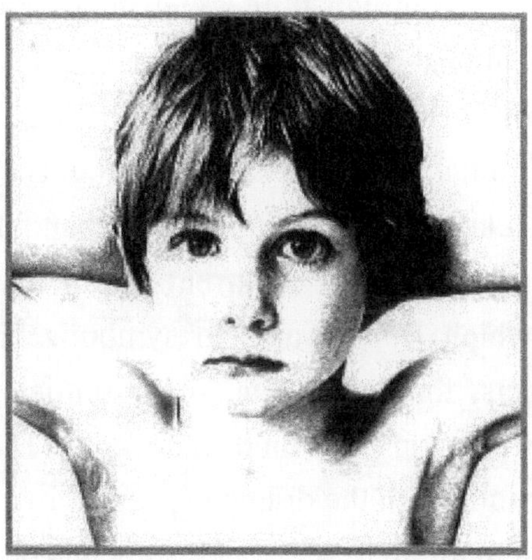

The band's early compositions are infused with spirituality and Christianity is both radical and revolutionary. The album was recorded in Windmill Lane Studios in Dublin. Some of the songs had already been played during the concerts before the works in the studio (as <u>Out of Control</u>, <u>Stories for Boys</u> and <u>Twilight</u>), other songs were born in the study (<u>An Cat Dubh/ Into the Heart</u> and <u>The Ocean</u>). The album treats of becoming an adult, a topic that serves as a common thread in the texts.

From the musical point of view, we are talking about being sophisticated and not spontaneous: Bono has the task of transmitting abandonment and passion, and he sings lyrics of innocence and failure, he sings the sadness with an obvious sentimentality ready to pierce any resistance, something that disrupts the non-believers.

It almost transpires a strong sense of urgency. We find a mixture of everyday and common things and things rather more bizarre, shadowy and almost menacing scenes are sung and proposed as if they were dark secrets too important to be lost. They are songs of extreme emotional insecurity and uncertainty. We can think the title 'Boy' as related to Bono, if not to the band itself: the absorbed imagination of a child, the recurrent use of the word 'boy' in the songs with which Bono wants to symbolize his confusion and thereby reflects, through music, the essential innocence of U2, which is now a decomposition of innocence. The sense of wonder becomes a unique with the drama expressed by the music.

Here starts a path that will lead somewhere in the future, or perhaps nowhere; it is not so easy to find what you want! The spiritual often appears in U2 and in these early works still appears even innocence, in contrast to what will be the subsequent work, more mature and less innocent and more steeped in consumerism and sin. Factors such as background, education, time and place are and will be decisive.

We talk about a psychological dance in which everything, every thought, every emotion continues to pirouette: the rock changes when it becomes a way to make self-consciousness, when people begin to see God in the music.

U2's music is so positive and optimistic that brings thoughts and emotions in the right direction and makes you follow it. From the first album they are clearly distinguishable from the Rolling Stones, who take the music of the devil and dress it in human clothes, while U2 begin to sing of innocence and pose the aim to change things and bring back all the way of the Spirit.

U2 rise from a sheltered musical life and influences by others joined them late so that they could grow naturally and staff. They are much more idealistic and stand up for one reason, just to speak out something important loud.

This album echoes of sounds and feelings that are entirely new: there's romance, the air of a dream that is offset by a new aggression, a new immediacy. No trace is radically different to the other in the building or in the plot, it is the new explosion of sounds introduced by U2 that reveal their cards and indicate the direction to take and follow. <u>Boy</u> will be considered by the fans an entirely introspective album, the research within himself of what then, in parallel, we should find in what surrounds us in the world.

<u>Boy</u> is a touching and innovative album, a mixture of archaic and modernist belief, a complex and multi-faceted album, as indeed will prove to be later albums. It still does not erase the thoughts that we may have towards this new band that wants to get ahead, but at least it strengthens affection for their character, and their music has an extraordinary emotional force. It is not radical, it is in many ways traditionalist, but it is honest, direct and wants to communicate, it wants to open minds and souls to convey a message without hiding any sign of complacency or silly certainty.

<u>*"I will follow"*</u> is definitely the most classic U2 song, the one that best emphasizes the references to religion and that introduces what will be even after the style and intention of the group.

In the verse "If you walk away walk away I will follow" we recognize the biblical reference in Ruth 1:16, "But Ruth said, 'Entreat me not to leave you or to return from following you; for where you go I will go, and where you lodge I will lodge; your people Shall be my people, and your God my God'.".

This song can be considered as the reference for all the faithful followers of Christ as well as a new force in the modern music coming from Ireland.

In an interview released for <u>Rolling Stone</u> Bono himself points out that this song is about "wonderful love". The Greeks had three ways to define love; wonderful love is unconditional love, like that we have for God is opposed to erotic love and to the friendly one.

Bono himself confirmed that <u>I will follow</u> is a song about his mother, but that is also a song about God.

Twilight still offers religious interpretations. How can we not read in the first verse the discovery of God? "I look into His Eyes/ they're closed but I see something": God is mystery, we can just catch a glimpse of Him but He is not easily revealed, as He is so difficult to understand. It 's like to see his eyes, trying to get in, to look at what lies beyond, but note that his eyes are closed.

Yet there is something that we can see the same... We cannot see God and we cannot investigate Him; we can only believe in what appears.

Still "my body grows and grows/ it frightens me you know/ the old man tried to walk me home" refers to how we grow more and more afraid. It refers that we grow and understand what the world is when we no longer see it through the eyes of a child. The old man who tries to bring us back to the house is none other than God, who wants to be on our side and try to bring us back to the right path through the maze of the world. This idea is reiterated in the next verses "Twilight, lost my way/ Twilight, can not find my way// In the shadow boy meets man": in the twilight we will lose the right way, but in the shadow boy meets man, because he learns to grow up and learns to understand that there is no God. The sense of twilight is in its being the boundary between day and night, between light and darkness, between good and evil. Nietzsche himself speaks of "Twilight of the Gods". In that case we speak of the end of all the gods that Man has created, the end of everything, until we get to nihilism; here we can feel the twilight as a crossroads in human life: on the one hand, the darkness, the evil, the death of God, on the other hand the light and God are with us to guide us.

Into the heart is, in my opinion, a statement made by God himself: in the heart of a child God can stand, stay and come back. The innocence of children allow it, their heart is still pure. Adulthood will be more difficult and not always there will be place for God in the hearts of Mankind.

In _Out of control_ we can find the clearest reference to God and religion in the verses "One day I'll die/ the choice will not be mine/ will it be too late/ you can not fight it": sooner or later everyone must die, but who is that man who has not died by his own choice? We are speaking about Christ. Christ was crucified not by his own choice, and at his death, on realizing that everything he had said was the truth, they realized also that it was too late and that there was nothing else to do.

In _Another time, another place_ the religious interpretation is a reverberation that affects the entire text: in the first strophe there is the abandonment, the waking up to find oneself alone and afraid. In the next strophe, then repeated several times as a refrain, the desire to reach those who are no more and the consciousness of being able to reach those who are no more. "Real life is on a cloud", in another time and in another place; in his life a child is defeated (there is evil with which he comes in contact when he grows, there is the loss of innocence) but the real life is in another place and at another time, and real life has a price.

Chapter 3

OCTOBER (Island 1981)

With this album the group members openly declare their devoutness. As <u>Boy</u> was the band's most Irish album now <u>October</u> is the most overtly religious. In 2001 it was added to the forty-first place in the ranking of the most Christians albums of CCM magazine. Later, <u>the Joshua tree</u> was added too.

The Edge himself says that the underlying problem was the label "Christian" and the fact they wanted to pursue their thinking and transmit it to others without being harassed by a label. The real problems are not with Christ, but with Christians and at that time the band was going through its greatest moment of spiritual growth. They were so involved to focus almost exclusively on that.

"Gloria" is the opening track and second single from the album. The song can be considered a direct result of the conversion to Catholicism of the band, with the exception of the atheist Adam to whom will be dedicated the song <u>Drowning Man</u> in the album <u>War</u>: God from the point of view of a non-believer. In the text there is a verse in Latin extracted from the liturgy, and it is the first U2 song that relates to a religious theme. Bono says in an interview how he was experiencing a period of artistic crisis and how therefore it came naturally to write the text of a prayer.

In verse "In te domine...exultate...miserere" is expressed the religious essence of the song. We find, in Latin, the first words of three psalms: Psalms 30 (31): "In Thee O Lord Do I put my trust..."; 32 (33): "Rejoice in the Lord, ye righteous..." e 50 (51): "Have mercy on me, O God".

Then there is an extra biblical quotation in verse "Only in you I am Complete": Colossians 2:10 "For in (Christ) dwells all the fullness of the Godhead bodily. And in Him you are complete".

Among the various interpretations it has also been pointed out how we can see in the passage a simple man, normal like all of us, who loves his religion and discovers that there's no need to know the right words to express the love to God. He wants to be with God in his Church but does not know the exact words ("I try, I try to speak up"), he does not know the courtly Latin used by the priests ("I try to sing this song"), so he tries to recite what he has heard and remembers.

But no matter what are the exact words, "the door is open", and the love to God can be expressed in every way.

Against the backdrop of the conflict between Irish Catholics and

Protestants, we can say that using the Latin Bono is almost invoking Catholicism. Indeed, the prayer of surrender to God and glorify God is pointing to some of the primary principles of the Christian and Protestant traditions and can be therefore, more than anything else, an attempt to follow the path through which these two traditions can learn from each other and can learn to respect each other instead of continuing to fight.

"I threw a brick through a window" is again imbued with religious interpretations. The verses "No one... no one is blinder/ than he who will not see/ No one... no one is blinder/ than me" suggest that Jesus preached His doctrine, but not all listen to Him and believe in Him. It makes we think how in front of much evidence that God has given us of His existence, yet we do not want to believe in Him; as blind men we do not see His presence: we are not really blind, rather we want to be blind; it is more convenient to hide our heads in the sand than recognize how things are. Bono is part of this blind humanity and he is the blindest of all. Many people realize that they must understand and believe in order to bring the message to others. Even stronger is the calling in the verses "Be my brother/ there is another way out of here/ in my brother" in which Bono invokes Jesus and asks Him to be his brother. There is only one way out to the world and can only be found in Christ, now brother.

Rejoice has already in the title its religiosity. "I'm falling" at the beginning of the song seems to be a cry of Satan falling from the sky while his fall disrupts and destroys the world. The "child on the ground" is Christ Himself Who is born in nothing but knows that He can fix everything and change the whole world. This is a cause for joy.

"I can't change the world/ but I can change the world in me/ if I rejoice" is the observation that a single man can never change the world, but he can change the world that he has inside, if he speaks with Christ and turns to His coming.

"Fire" openly refers to the Apocalypse: "The sun is burning black ... the moon is running red ... the stars are falling down" is a clear recovery of the Book of Revelation 6, 24:13: "Then I watched while he broke open the sixth seal, and there was a great earthquake; the sun turned as black as dark sackcloth and the whole moon became like blood. The stars in the sky fell to the earth like unripe figs shaken loose from the tree in a strong wind". At that time, Bono was deeply torn between his faith and his commitment to the music. Could faith and music be reconciled? Or had he to choose one rather than the other? The song deals with this too, deals with the revelation that is almost denied to Bono and with the impression that going on with the music would have turned him away from God and condemned to hell. The reference to the hell that surrounds him is clear: "Fallen! Fallen is Babylon the Great! "(Revelation 18:2).

If we interpret the song in relation to Bono's personal experience and thus analysing every reference according to Bono's own life comes back still vividly his inner conflict: in the reflection of the world to come (in the images of the darkened sun, the fiery moon and the stars falling from the sky) we can see the uncertainty of the future and the uncertainty to make right choices in order not to fall into the same fate Babylon fell.

"Tomorrow" is the sixth track on the album and together with I Will Follow and then Lemon and Mofo was written in memory of his dead mother. Here in particular we are in the day of the funeral of the woman.

We can find biblical references in the line "Who tore the curtain? Who was it for?" that takes the words of the crucifixion (Matt 27:51): "At that moment the curtain of the temple was torn in two from top to bottom. The earth shook and the rocks split".

The image of the door and "open up to the Lamb of God" is taken from Revelation 3:20 where Jesus says: "Behold, I stand at the door, and knock: if any man hear my voice, and open the door, I will come in to him, and will eat with him, and he with me".

So if on one hand we can read the anger of a boy who has lost his mother, the anger of a boy who does not understand how God can take away his most important person and screams his rage in pain, on the other hand we can see in the song the end of the world and the second coming of Christ to bring along his followers. And when the boy will be with God he will be with his mother again.

"October" is one of the shortest songs (only a little over a minute), but its meaning is very deep. "And kingdoms rise and kingdoms fall" can be found in Psalm 46:6 "Nations are in uproar, kingdoms fall; he lifts His voice, the earth mealts".

It highlights how nothing on earth will last forever, but through God the spirit will continue forever to be alive.

Just as in October things die, life has also its own cycle of death and rebirth. Time passes and things happen, we are spectators and part of this cycle. Only God is outside, where there is no beginning and no end.

Also note as October is the month of Samhain, or Halloween, which is celebrated in Ireland and Scotland as "late summer". According to the Celtic tradition we may honour the dead and open a new beginning in the cycle of life. Thus <u>October</u> is an exhortation to move forward, it talks about what continues to be and whispers of a new beginning after the loss of what we held dear.

<u>*With a Shout*</u>: the Biblical reference is already in the title (Psalm 47:5 "God has gone up with a shout, the Lord with the sound of a trumpet").

"Mount Zion" was the hill where it was built the Temple of God; "Son of Zion," thus refers to the chosen people while "Daughter of Zion" is Jerusalem itself. The reference is Isaiah 2:1-5: "In the days to come the mountain of the Lord's house shall be established as the highest of the mountains, and shall be raised above the hills. All the nations shall stream to it".

In the reference to the hill and the blood poured from it we find the reference to the crucifixion. We fall at the feet of the Messiah, on that hill, at the foot of the man who opens the eyes of mankind to the truth, and at the foot of the hill we stay still to be filled by love.

Even in an instrumental piece as _"Scarlet"_ (as it had already happened in <u>Rejoice</u>) it can be found the main theme of religiosity: Bono reiterates the notion that his faith is not a stereotype but a feeling, rooted in his culture and in his education in Ireland.

"Stranger in a strange land" was written when Bono and the band went to Berlin and describes their emotion in front of a soldier guarding the border between the two Germanies (the stranger and the strange land). We can, however, read in it the allusion to the story of Emmaus (Luke 24), where Jesus appears as a foreigner and is not recognized until it gives the bread to the disciples. The song paraphrases their exclamation after recognizing Him: "Were not our hearts burning within us while he talked with us on the road and opened the Scriptures to us?" In the lyrics are "I watched as he watched us. The way it was when he was with us". The disciples did not go to sleep but they went to tell what happened and how the Lord had risen and they recognized Him. We can read this in the lines "But I could not sleep after what I saw: I wrote this letter to tell you the way I feel. I wish you were here to see what I could see ".
With the invocation "I wish you were here" we feel the need for someone stronger who can be a witness to what is happening, perhaps in order to realize how things really are here and to be able to intervene.

Chapter 4

WAR (Island, 1983)

The religiosity carried by <u>October</u> now flows in <u>War</u> even if this new album carries a deep political message. This is also the album that consecrates U2 to the world.

<u>War</u> is a record that wants to reflect on the psychological consequences of warfare in the way we approach life. In those years, the information was definitely evolving, so it was easier to know about the present conflict everywhere in the world. We are now spectators of events. This observation by the Dubliner group will become the pin in <u>Achtung Baby</u>. With <u>War</u> opens U2's pacifist-political season . The first three tracks on the disc hit like punches and leverage those emotions that arise from the absurd consequences of the war: <u>Sunday Bloody Sunday</u> refers to the famous Bloody Sunday of the Bogside Massacre of 1972, <u>Seconds</u> is about nuclear proliferation and the risks it implies, while <u>New Year's Day</u> is linked to the solidarity movement in Poland. In the last track <u>40</u>, with the text taken directly from Psalm 40 of the

Bible, that religious theme so dear to the Irish band in future albums emerges.

The disc is in effect new and forerunner while remaining completely accessible to anyone to make them understand that perhaps they will not be able to change the world but this is certainly a start and hope is alive.

"Sunday bloody Sunday" is a strong and controversial song: it is often read as a rebellious song while it is in fact a song that calls for peace. The song refers to the "bloody Sunday", on the 30th January 1972, when the royal army shot on the crowd in the north-Irish city of Derry and 14 people were shot dead. At that time Bono was only a child and this fact left an everlasting mark on him.

Bono himself makes clear that <u>Sunday bloody Sunday</u> is not a song of rebellion but it is the incredulous reaction of a young man who has grown up in an interfaith family in the Irish Republic facing the hate and violence that divide those who might be one in the name of Christ. The repeated question "how long must we sing this song?" will be then resumed in the song <u>40</u> at the end of the album ("how long to sing this song") as a supplication to God and to His intervention.

There are many biblical references in this song to witness that even the most political song does not miss the band's religiosity.

"Trenches dug within our hearts, and mothers, children, brothers, sisters torn apart" is taken from Matthew, 10:35: "For I have come to set a man against his father, a daughter against her mother, and a daughter-in-law against her mother-in-law".

"Wipe the tears from your eyes" is almost a paraphrase of a line from the Book of Revelation: Revelation 21:4: "He will wipe every tear from their eyes".

"We eat and drink while tomorrow they die" is once more a brilliant biblical interpretation: Corinthians 15:32: "If the dead are not raised, let us eat and drink, for tomorrow we die".

Last but not less important is the refrain "How long must we sing this song". The shout "how long" is very recurring all through the Bible, but here particularly we must underline

- Psalm 6:3 "My soul is in anguish. How long. O Lord, how long?" (that, according to Bono himself, will be drawn up in 40 too).

- Psalm 94:3: "How long will the wicked, o Lord, how long will the wicked be jubilant?"

- Abacuc 1:2: "How long, o Lord, must I call for help, but you do not listen? Or cry out to you, "Violence!" but you do not save?"

"Seconds" : Bono himself says (New Musical Express, 1983): "Before we can defeat these things we have to deal with them. There is a verse in Seconds which speaks of a fanatic who assembles a nuclear device in an apartment in Times Square, New York, but it could be anywhere. We are entering the era of nuclear terrorism where a group of fanatics might have the ability to carry a bomb in a city and hold hostage millions of people".

Even here, however, is visible the religious reference in the verse "like a thief in the night" which is in the Bible "for you know very well that the day of the Lordwill come like a thief in the night".

(I Thessalonians 5:2)

New Year's Day" is a song that sings of the desire to be with God, of the will to be always the same as before and continue, as before, to be with Him.

There is an observation, almost the proof that God exists: "The newspaper says, says/ it's true it's true..." are verses that appear immediately after the story of how a crowd of a few selected people meets (and then is saved) under a blood red sky (i.e. the Day of Judgement).

"And we can break through/ though torn in two/ we can be one" are verses that sing of the possibility, in God, to be a single entity. Although divided (because of belief, race, or whatever reason), by finding themselves in God and starting again in God it is possible to be united and at peace.

In the last strophe we find once again the willingness to choose God rather than the world: we are told that we live in an age when wealth is more important than all the other values, an age in which man fights for wealth, yet for the singer still remains the power to choose God and communicate it to the world.

"Like a song" is a song that, even in its most purely political meaning, hides an hymn and a prayer to God.

In the opening lines we can read the desire to offer the song to God and to offer Him the words we has to say: "Like a song I have to sing I sing it for you/ Like the words I have to bring I bring it for you".

In the lines "And you know I do not believe/ too young to be told/

exactly who are you/ tonight/ tomorrow 's too late", the sadness of realizing how in youth, even not believing, there is no way to change this state just because too young for this and unable to understand who God really is and everything He can. Of course the concept of infinity, which is God, is too big to be conceived and understood by the human mind that, as such, has a limit and a boundary. Growing up at least we get to understand that there is someone we can rely on and who accompanies us on our journey. It is now too late, however: when we understand the true values we have already been taken into the vortex of life, with its wars and its revolutions.

"But I won't.../ let others live in hell" is the desire to shout to everyone that there is something more, that believing in something higher can improve life. The message must be carried to everyone.

Other very significant lines are "and if you can't help yourself/ well take a look around you": in them we read that we alone are not enough to ourselves and we need to seek help all around. Help can come from both the outside world in dedicating oneself to others so that by helping them we help ourselves, and from something else that is around us. There is a constant presence that allows us not to be alone and to find ourselves. Everything culminates with the last lines of the song, where we find an invocation to God: "A new heart is what I need/ oh God, make it bleed" in which we recognize "I will give you a new heart and put a new spirit in you; I will remove from you your heart of stone and give you a heart of flesh" (Ezekiel 36:26). Hence the need for a new heart that bleeds (can we see in these lines also a parallel with Christ and with His bleeding heart, pierced on the Cross? It is simply to have Christ in us, as our heart). This is the only solution. To be like Christ and with Christ to spread a new message of change.

"Drowning man" is, like the eye of the storm, a song of hope and faith in the midst of an album centred on the theme of war.
In this song is God Who speaks and aims at those who do not trust in Him and do not want to believe in Him Men who drown, the "lost", are in crisis with their faith, but with the help of Christ they discover and convince themselves that God's Love is eternal. As already mentioned, the song is almost a dedication to Adam, the atheist of the group, that not believing in God becomes part of the group of lost people and here represents that group. Later, in the song "Peace on Earth", we still find a reference to the "drowning man": "Jesus can you take the time/ to throw a drowning man a line/ peace on earth..." and yet there is a clear sense of inner battle that, considering what surrounds us in life and in the world, can only be won with the help of Jesus.
To return to the shore who is lost, God offers His help; more: He offers to reach out across the sky trying to persuade the Man to grab it and believe in Him. Nothing will threaten those who are with God, Who is a safe haven in the storm.
"Hold on, hold on tightly/ to this love... last forever" is the latest attempt by God to convince the Man to cling to Him because His Love is eternal, nothing can undermine It unlike what is the world in which we live, always so unstable and changeable that can only lead to drift if we are alone.

We can find the confirmation of all that in the lines "Rise up, rise up/ with wings like eagles/ you'll run, you'll run/you'll run and not grow weary" in which the reference to Isaiah 40: 31 is clear: "but those who hope in the Lord will renew their strength. They will soar on wings like eagles; they will run and not grow weary, they will walk and not be faint".

The "drowning man" can also be connected to the biblical episode in which Jesus invites Peter to walk on water and try to reach Him so to prove his faith. Removed his eyes from Jesus, Peter sees the stormy waters and begins to sink. Jesus takes him by the hand, the storm dies down, and together they reach the boat.

More and more emphasis is placed on the concept that the removal from Jesus (and thus from faith) plunges us into the storm (both moral and intimate in which we can see the difficulties of life), but with the help of Jesus (and therefore of faith) we can find comfort and salvation.

"Two hearts beat as one" is a song certainly more sentimental than religious, but why don't we see the two hearts as those of God and the believer that beat as one in faith?

In the lines "Say I'm a fool/ you say I'm not for you/ but if I'm a fool for you/ oh, that's something" we recognize references to "If any one among you seems to be wise in this world, let him become a fool, that he may be wise" (I Corinthians 3:18), and even more," We are fools for Christ's sake "(I Corinthians 4:10).

Red Light is a song that, once more, can be read as a dialogue between God and someone who can be everyone.

God offers His help, He let us know how people depart when they hear His Words because they fear. They seem to depart to run away from themselves.

"I give you my love/ still you walk away" is a strong observation: God gives us all His Love, He has done this by sacrificing His Son for our salvation, He always does this by being with us and inside us to support us. Despite all this we try to depart from Him, we think to have no need for others to face the "tragedy" that is life itself, so bristling with obstacles and temptations. We run away from a God that is Goodness and Love almost because we fear Him so much He is great and because of all the love He can give us.

"Surrender" is once more a song based on the struggle to keep firm Christian laws: Faith always wavers facing the world and its difficulties.

In Bono's mind the idea of "city" stretches very often on that of "world". The world is full of lovers and lies and the biggest lie is to negate the existence of God.

Sadie is the main character of the song, but she could be everyone. She never thought about the existence of a God and she never asked herself about the reason why she is here on the earth: she simply lives her life as anyone can live his own life committing himself to doing its best and to living at its best, but it is not always so easy to understand the real sense of what we do and the real sense of life itself. We realize only later that without a final destination or a particular call life loses its sense, but sometimes we must reach a last point to understand it: Sadie is ready to jump from the forty-eighth floor when Bono tells her to let herself go. Not go to the empty space under her, but let herself go to God.

However difficult is in the world to stop and think about God it is only if He holds us His hand out and we let ourself go to Him that we can overcome difficulties: life, the world, are always lying in wait to take what we have built and above all to take all the goodness that we have in us.

Luke 9: 24-25 "For whoever wishes to save his life will lose it, but whoever loses his life for my sake will save it. What profit is there for one to gain the whole world yet lose or forfeit himself?" becomes in the song "If I wanna live I gotta die to myself, someday". Jesus says that to reach eternal life everyone has to die and carry its own cross; in a so wrong world we have in us something that is always present and alive, it is the love we express and that comes to us from God, the love that is always addressed to Him. Life has its own price and the price is just death. With the death we can understand the real meaning of life and come back to God, in Love.

_"40"_ is the musical rendering of Psalm 40, even if Bono himself declares in his introduction to the book of Psalms that the verse "How long (to sing this song)" is taken from Psalm 6.

The song is extracted as the last single from the album War. It was recorded the last night that the band had at his disposal the recording studio. They still missed a song to close the album, Adam had already returned home and so they decided to record a song with only the bass guitar (played by Edge) and with a text taken on the moment. The choice fell on Psalm 40 because it well accorded with the project of the band: a highly spiritual text to close an album with a strong political impact.

In his <u>Introduction to the Book of Psalms</u> Bono notes how for a band like theirs was considered almost a taboo to use the Scriptures in this way unless it was "in the service of Satan" (in opposition with the blues and the gospel of black people). The text of Psalm 40 strikes Bono very much because it suggests a moment when grace will replace karma, and love will take the place of the iron laws of Moses. <u>40</u> has been for long the closing track to the U2 shows, with the audience repeating endlessly the refrain.

"How long to sing this song" takes us back to "How long must we sing this song" of <u>Sunday Bloody Sunday</u> and reappears in the song, perhaps the more strictly religious song of the band, the reference to the political theme: the irony of people who kill in the name of religion. God does not need us to fight His battles in His place because His will is perfect and we are not asked to make it so.

This is seen as a tormenting question addressed to an invisible deity we glimpse at only when we act in love.

Psalm 40 is centred on patience. Through all the Scriptures the number 40 symbolizes patience: we find the forty days and nights of the flood, forty days in the desert, and so on.

Still, we can make of this song a song about the experience of conversion: "brought up from a pit" that is in regaining faith we come out of the pit into which we he had fallen without God.

"How long to sing this song" still fits in the experience of conversion, as it can refer to the fact that throughout his life the Christian is called to sing hymns to God, to sing a new song that will teach many others to see and fear, to seek God and find Him among the evils of the world.

The refrain can also be read as a cry addressed to God, asking how long we still have to sing the same song, continuing to demand the end of the pain and suffering. How long have we to wait for God and salvation with Him?

We understand how far we are from God, because He knows everything about us while we, in our sinful human beings, will never fill up the gap that separates us from Him. He knows the future as well as we ignore it. "I will sing a new song" underlines that there is something good in human nature; it is the desire to go on seeking God even in the evil that surrounds us. We are responsible for our actions and we must choose to remain positive despite everything and wait thus our reward if we have the patience to wait for God ("waiting patiently for the Lord").

Chapter 5

THE UNFORGETTABLE FIRE
(Island, 1984)

This is the first U2 album to enter "Billboard"'s Top Ten and it is the turning point of the entire career of the band, which emphasizes its social commitment. The songs speak of the crisis and disappointment of America because of the failure to achieve its ideals. The "Unforgettable Fire" is that of the atomic bomb, but the theme of war is put alongside with other issues as ever: the new theme of drug, hymns to the great personalities of the time, spirituality.

The association with Brian Eno and Daniel Lanois begins with this album, and immediately we notice their influence with the introduction and use of a more evocative sound

The unforgettable fire is definitely more mature and "grown-up" than the previous albums.

In _A sort of homecoming_ we can read the consciousness that at the end of the evil, the sufferings and the storms that we go through there is a light that shines in the distance and waits for us; it is peace and joy; it is God.

Despite this awareness, we are at a boundary and we see that on one side there is the possibility to get better (which coincides with the desire to feel better that we have inside). It's not easy to go towards this positivity, because there is always something that draws us into evil and suffering, we remain in the balance on the border.

A strophe sings "On borderland we run/ and still we run/ we run and do not look back/ I'll be there/ I'll be there/ tonight/ tonight/ I'll be there tonight... I believe" and with these words emphasizes the ride along this border and the willingness to go towards the Good. Right on the end it highlights, however, the uncertainty that characterizes us and makes us falter, leaving us suspended.

At the end of all this the Good prevails and we find that it is possible to go on the right side, out of the standstill: "I'll be there somehow.../ I'll be there tonight..." is the consciousness that we can find a way to go. The concept is reaffirmed in lines "Tonight we'll build a bridge/ across the sea and land": by building a bridge to overcome obstacles a connection is created, a secure bond that allows us to move from the border and lead us in the right direction.

"Don't sorrow, don't weep/ for tonight, at last/ I am coming home" want to be the confirmation that we have finally found the way. Is it maybe to God that the singer turns when he asks not to be sad? The Man has found his way, he overcame the temptations and the evils that surround him and can now return to that which is his home, in the Peace, towards the light.

In _"Pride"_, even if Bono himself declares that the song is dedicated to Martin Luther King Jr, we can clearly recognize the biblical quotations and the religious readings.

How not to associate "one man betrayed with a kiss" to the biblical verse "Jesus said to him, 'Judas, are you betraying the Son of Man with a kiss?'"? And again, "one man washed on an empty beach" is a possible reference to Jonah 2:10: "Then the Lord ordered the fish to spit Jonah up on the beach, and it did".

"One man come he to justify" is taken from Isaiah 53:11, which is probably the most well-known prophecy about the coming of Christ: "my righteous servant will justify many, and he will bear their iniquities.". "Justify" is a key verb in Christian theology which refers to how the grace of Jesus takes the believers closer to God.

"One man come in the name of love" is certainly MLK bearing his message of love and justice, but is also Christ Jesus the Man Who comes in the name of love, Who is the Name of Love, Love made flesh, God made Man...

"One man come and go" is MLK who has come to shout his message to the people and than has gone, killed, but it is also Christ who has come on the earth and has conquered it with His message, and has come back home to live for eternity.

"One man come, he to justify" is once more Christ who has come to redeem His people charging to Himself the sins and faults. Faith in Christ redeems Christians.

"One man to overthrow" is MLK struggling to overcome the prejudices and discriminations, but is also Christ Who defeats Satan's kingdom by destroying the one who has in himself the power of death with His own death on the cross.

"In the name of love/ what more in the name of love": what more could be done in the name of love? MLK died for his fight and for the message he wanted to leave, just as God has let His Son die on the cross to save mankind from sin. The world hated Jesus so much to want Him killed, but He has never stopped to love the world .

"One man caught on a barbed wire fence" is a metaphor for the cross, the reference to the crown of thorns.

"One man he resist" is Christ who resists the temptations of Satan.

"One man washed on an empty beach" is a reference to the baptism of John, but it's also the isolation of Christ on the cross: no one took pity on Him and he found Himself alone to face death.

"One man betrayed with a kiss" is a clear reference to Jesus betrayed by the kiss of Judas.

This whole section can be considered as an hymn to Christ and to His sacrifice for humanity.

The conclusion refers again equally to MLK and Christ at once. "Free at last, they took your life They could not take your pride": both the life of MLK and that of Christ have been broken, but their message of freedom and love lives on.

In _"Wire"_ we turn to Judah with reference to the betrayal committed against Jesus.

At the beginning there is the awareness of being both innocent and guilty for the death of Jesus because, as Men, we are sinners and therefore we have condemned Jesus to death, but at the same time, as Men, we have believed in Him and we have not physically put Him on the cross.

"Watch you tear yourself apart" is a closer reference to Judah: we know that he is guilty, whereas before the betrayal he was a friend of Jesus. We are thus watching him as he is torn apart by the consciousness of his guilt.

The fourth strophe sings "So lay me down/ my soul to give/ so lay me down/ the longest sleep" and it is a turning to God to ask Him to give us the eternal sleep: Man is aware that Jesus is betrayed and unfairly sentenced, but doing nothing to prevent His death makes him so much guilty to beg for death. He feels unworthy of life.

Further on we find once again a strong reference to Judas and to the betrayal: "Any time you're on there/ (Kiss me...)/ won't you do it now?". The man who betrays can be anyone that comes our way and tries to move us away from the true value. It is expected that someone always betrays.

In the last strophe we find the lines "Cut throath let out/ I'm on your side/be on the both side" which are referred to how those who are in the wrong stay free as if they were innocent, but we are indeed on their same side even if we cannot be completely in evil: something pushes us to be on the side of Good too.

At the end of the song there is perhaps the strongest reference to the story of Judah: "I give you hope/ here's the rope/.../... Now swing away". There is hope for the betrayers too and the hope is given by death. With the hanging, Judah acknowledges his fault and by expiating his fault with death he finds the hope of salvation once again. So it must be for everyone, there is always hope, this is THE message.

"The unforgettable fire": the title is taken from an exhibition of paintings made by survivors of Hiroshima, even if the lyrics talk about a love story and there can be find religious references.
"And if the mountain should crumble or disappear into the sea" is a reference to Psalm 46:2 "Therefore we will not fear, though the earth give way and the mountains fall into the heart of the sea".
In "Face to face/ In a dry and waterless place" we find echoes of Psalm 63:1 "O God, you are my God; earnestly I seek you, my soul thirsts for you, my flesh faints for you, as in a dry and weary land where there is no water" but we can recognize it also in Deuteronomy 8:15 "He led you through the vast and dreadful desert, that dry and waterless land".
Even the verse "Red wine that punctures the skin" can be read in a religious sense: why do not interpret it as a reference to the crucifixion or to the Communion itself?

"Promenade" is full of verses that lead to a religious interpretation.
In the verse "Is she coming back again" we can perhaps recognize once again the identification of the Holy Spirit with a female figure: tied to the first verse of the song it is wondering if she will

return among us, from the depths from which it came, to guide us.
"Words that build or destroy" is a reference to the words of God: through the power of His Will He can create and destroy. He needs not much, just a word.

"Barbed-wire fence cut me down" speaks of the barbed wire that can kill. How can we not read in this verse the parallel with the crown of thorns of Jesus?

It is like asking that this very crown, because of the symbol that represents, kills us as sinners and guilty, to atone for our sins and return to the right. It is hoped to be raised to a higher level, closer to God: "I'd like to be around/ in a spiral staircase/ to the higher ground": the verses express at their best the desire to be among those who, through a tortuous and difficult way, reach THE higher place, THE higher level. The one where God is.

Even _"Indian Summer Sky"_ is full of echoes of spirituality. The beginning of the song is about how someone lost in the ocean or in the forest can finally see the light: are not these metaphors for the world, with its intricate difficulties, and for God, the light, towards which we run to find refuge and support?

"I run there towards the light" is the phrase.

"In the earth a hole dig deep, decide/ if I could, I would/ up to air to swim against the tide" describe very well how in facing a deep hole (thus the hell that sinks into the ground as opposed to heaven) it's up to us alone to decide whether to let ourselves fall down or fall back to the surface, breathe, swim against the current, against the temptations toward the light.

The concept of conversion and awareness of the right way is

reaffirmed with the simple phrase "the seasons change and so do I": it is with the changing of the seasons, with the growth and the evolution of mind and thought that we change, that we can figure out what is really important. We can also learn to choose Good trying to turn away from evil.

"The light that waits for I/ the light... waiting/ up toward the sky/ it's a blue sky" express the consciousness of the choice. The light expects every single "I". There's no obligation towards the light, but it is there waiting and we know it, we tend to it knowing that it will take us up into the sky, blue and clear as the grace and the purity. Upwards towards God.

"Elvis Presley and America" looks almost like a dialogue with God, or rather God speaking to someone, anyone.

"Black flash over my own love" emphasizes how God sees that His love is darkened, how the temptations can remove the believer from Him. God is a white glow that cleaves the sky, in contrast to what darkens Him, and He well knows the sadness that dwells in those far away from Him: "and your heart/ so cold when I'm with you" emphasizes once again the separation from God: He is there and He is with us, but we are cold with Him, we do not want to recognize Him and want to go on following our own way. There is a further confirmation of these words in the verses "Though no one told you/ and you found out/ where you were going, where to/ you're through with me/ but I know you will be back/ for more" in reaffirming that we consciously choose our path and follow it, but there is hope: God knows that it is to Him that we will return just because we always want more, and only He can give it to us. After all it is He Who faces our problems in our place and thus allows us to overcome them.

In saying "Me, I'm on the outside, tell me fade away/ drop me down but do not break me" we notice how God is always outside of us, He watches our lives and our choices without interfering. He asks only to be put aside but not broken, left to sink somewhere as a useless thing because sooner or later we will need Him, we will need His love that is always by our side. "So let me in your heart" is the only request that God gives us.

There is a way to get closer to God and we know it: "You know S.O.N.G., why/ you're going go join to God" means, in the song, that now is the time of death; we can more broadly interpret "join to God" not as death, but as life. A new life with Him because we have found Him again.

There is a way and we know it: just a SONG, right words (and choices) and we will be with Him again.

In the end of the song is once more underlined the return to God: "If you pick me up/ bits and pieces on this floor" makes the idea of something that has been first thrown away and then picked up: it is our original renunciation to God to retrace than our steps and try to rebuild our relationship with Him.

Chapter 6

THE JOSHUA TREE (Island, 1987)

After three years of absence from the scene comes out the perhaps most memorable U2 album. Great were the expectations for the new job and the expectations were not only met but also exceeded.

It's definitely the album of maturity, where the best vocals of Bono are merged with the technological element of Brian Eno and the usual basis of the band that always frames the lyrics. With this record, U2 are closer to America, in sounds as in look and blend their traditional sounds with echoes of blues and country ballads.

The light of the Faith in Christ still stands as a shining light on the band in this album.

In the album the three pillars of the music of U2 are perfectly merged: we have the gospel moaning and religiosity, the elegies of love and political denunciations. To these themes is now added the theme of drug abuse, a new analysis of another wrath of a society where the true values are lost to make room for more and new temptations.

The album title refers to a giant cactus that grows in the Death Valley, renamed Joshua by the early Mormons who came to America, as if they wanted a comparison between that place and the land promised by Joshua. But why not think to "The Joshua Tree" as "The Tree of Jesus" and see it as a symbol of the Christian Cross, to emphasize once more the religiosity inherent in the songs of the album?

From the words of Bono: "The real strength of this album is that it passes through dark tunnels and desolate landscapes, but at the centre of it all is joy".

<u>*"Where the streets have no name"*</u> is inspired by the journey made by Bono in Ethiopia with his wife following the LIVE AID. Bono explained that he was told how in Belfast it is possible to understand the richness and importance of a person depending on the street in which it lives as well as from the side of the road where it has its home. To counter all this he began to write of nameless streets .

The text written by Bono swings between sense of escape and hope.

"I want to feel sunlight on my face" is the desire to hear God Himself, the only real light in a place where we do not need another light and the roads do not need a name. Let's look at the last chapters of the Book of Revelation in which we can find a description of the world after the coming of the Antichrist: a new heaven and a new earth will arise and a new city will descend from heaven adorned with jewels. There will be no space neither for worship nor to give names to anything because God alone is the Temple.

In this song we can read of the New Jerusalem ("Heaven on Heart" as said further), which is located in the desert, where the streets have no name. We read this in the verses:

And when I go there	Towards the New Jerusalem
I go there with you	Jesus Christ will be with me
It's all I can do	There is no alternative to Faith to reach salvation.

"We are beaten and blown by the wind" is found in James 1:6 "But he should ask in faith, not doubting, for the one who doubts is like a wave of the sea that is driven and tossed about by the wind".

In the deluxe edition of the album we find a change to the original text: "I want to reach out and touch the flame" becomes "I've got to break out... holy spirit like a flame" and it seems to show how the Kingdom of God is the subject of the song.

It can be said that the modern era and its influence on those which are moral values, the real ones, are also expressed through the continuous construction: buildings, new shops and roads. In the song we find the verses "we're still building/ then burning down love" that underline how going on building we destroy the love;

how in the new society of consumerism and distinctions remains no more space for love, then for God.

"I still haven't found what I'm looking for" is almost a question about the difficulty on the part of the believer to hold fast to the faith in God.

The song is in perfect continuity with the previous one; here the certainty of faith coexists with the uncertainty of the doubt. The faith here leads through a journey of discovery that is often shrouded in darkness but always sustained by hope, which is an inner strength.

We still have a song that brings up what is the inability to give up the fundamental requirement that is the heart (and the reason) of Man: every human attempt to get to the mystery remains unanswered, but the Man cannot avoid going on to try, cannot give up the Ultimate Truth. The Man is conscious he will not ever get there, he can just try to get closer but he must try.

The song sings of the road to eternal life: there is all the journey that we humans are called to do in our search for God. All earthly things will not fill what our spirits really wants, but God has shown us the Grace. And the song says that God has broken the ties that bind us anchored to this world through His Son Jesus Christ, Who has carried the cross for all our sins and shames to set ourselves free. Here there is also the reference to a sentence of C.S. Lewis: "If I find in myself a desire which no experience in the world can satisfy, the most plausible explanation is that I was made for another world". And again we find a reminder of the Psalms, the song of ascent: Christians must understand that they can have a real relationship with God only fighting, as once Israel managed to do to have the true relationship with God. Now Bono tells us that he believes in God and in all that He said, but still can not "feel" it. And the search for this presence goes on, since he was a child, through the age of maturity, until the end.

In "I have spoken with the tongue of angels" we recognize the biblical reference to I Corinthians 13:1 "If I speak in the tongues of men and of angels, but have not love, I am only a resounding gong or a clanging cymbal".

*_With or without you_* is perhaps the most famous song and lends itself to various interpretations. It has a universal value, always appropriate in every circumstance and to what we want emotionally express, whether it is feelings (from love to hate) or the search for God.

The more mystical interpretation is taken from the complex and felt relationship and that Bono has with religion. Considering throughout the whole album we can consider With or without you the closing song of a triptych with Where the streets have no name and I still have not found what I'm looking for, a trinity whose theme is the search for a calm and balanced relationship with God. "See the thorn twist in your side" is 2 Corinthians 12:7: "To keep me from becoming conceited because of these surpassingly revelations, there was given me a thorn in my flesh, a messenger of Satan, to torment me".

The song is ultimately about Jesus. In the quoted verse Bono feels so close to Christ to feel like a witness to His death and to be now waiting for His return ("I wait for you").

In the verse "On a bed of nails she makes me wait" Bono refers to the Holy Spirit as a "she", as happens also in other songs (see for example <u>Mysterious ways</u> where we find "She moves in mysterious ways") and is "She" that accompanies us, almost like a lover, in the journey through Hell up to God. He sings of a relationship between two people, but the partner is now the Holy Spirit, a "She", and because of this it is easier to explain the concept of relationship: the condition of being human implies the need to find someone to save us from loneliness and at some point we find someone, or, rather, that Someone who confronts us with the choice to "live with or without Him". And the pain is Hell.

The verse "and you give yourself away" reminds us once again to Christ rather than to an hypothetical partner, it makes sense to think that the one who "gives himself away" is Christ who gives His life for the salvation of Man.

The verse "Through the storm we reach the shore" is another biblical allusion: it is easy to relate it to the story of Peter, when Christ calms the stormy waters and walking on the same they reach the quiet beach. The Man knows and recognizes the miracles of Christ, but that's not enough: to make the faith stronger and more concrete we need something more ("I want more") and we can only wait.

Anger emerges from the song, the anger of someone who realizes that he can not live neither with nor without God, there is certainly faith, there is religion and so on, but at the same time we are doomed to be human with all that this entails. Hence the difficulty in having a relationship with God: certainly it has not been easy for Christ to carry His cross, but it is the more difficult for us. But is there really God? We can not avoid to believe it, because a life without God is difficult, but is it really so easy to live with Him, with all that He asks us to do in His name?

The song can also be read the other way: it is Jesus who speaks to us from the cross:

"See the stone set in your eyes/ see the thorn twist in your side/ I wait for you" is the image of Christ Who wears the crown of thorns and to Whom are thrown stones, but nevertheless expects His executioners.

"Slide of hand and twist of fate/ on a bed of nails she makes me wait/ and I wait without you": there is the betrayal of Judas that changes the destiny of things. "She" becomes a reference to his mother Mary, Who sees Him crucified and knows that His Son should wait on a bed of pain without Her, without a comfort.

"Through the storm we reach the shore/ you give it all but I want more/ and I'm waiting for you" becomes here the message of God and of Christ: through the adversities of life He is there and it is through Him that we can defeat evil, sin and adversity to achieve peace. We commit ourselves to live better through Christ, but still is not enough, more is needed, and God is waiting for us, He waits that we look to Him and wants our love while we have always His. "My hands are tied/ My body bruised, she's got me with/ nothing to win/ and nothing left to lose" is still Christ who speaks to us from the cross, His hands are tied, the battered body is dying ("she" is now clearly the death that takes Him away with it) and there is nothing left to win or to lose, the fate is accomplished, He has given Himself to humanity and now waits for us.

"Bullet the blue sky" is a song inspired by a trip that Bono made in Central America in 1985. Though the song is more properly political, it contains biblical references and has also religious interpretations: "See it driving nails/ Into the souls on the tree of pain" refers to the crucifixion; the tree of pain is nothing but the cross, the only thing to which we can be nailed. But the nails pierce not only Christ on the cross, they pierce also the souls, the souls of those who live in pain because of their sins, those who only Christ can redeem through His death.

"Jacob wrestled the angel/ And the angel was overcome" is from Genesis 32:25: "Jacob was left there alone. Then some man wrestled with him until the break of dawn". After the battle, Jacob was called Israel and his twelve sons became the twelve tribes of Israel, the people of God.

"You plant a demon seed/ you raise a flower of fire" stresses how from a sin ("the demon seed") derives only pain and negativity (even a flower, usually a symbol of joy and also of purity, becomes "flower of fire", a symbol of pain and fear that makes us think of hell). The verses can be thought of in relation to the original sin of Adam and Eve ("the seed") that has slowly grown to give rise to all the evils of the world ("the demon flower"). Even the crosses that burn with higher and higher flames refer to the new fall of humanity in a state of sin and separation from the true values of religion: they burn crosses, ultimate religious symbol, and they watch the flames that become higher; it is the destruction of the faith and the desire to reach the sky with flames to challenge the heaven itself and tell everybody that there's nobody there. At the same time, the image of the burning cross makes us think of a characteristic image of Christianity, the well known "flaming heart", in which a cross surmounts a heart surrounded by thorns and burns with it: it is the sacrifice of Jesus that saves us from sin and opens the way to forgiveness and to Heaven.

In _"Running to stand still"_ Bono deals with the sensitive problem of drug abuse and he is inspired by a true story happened in his hometown, Dublin.

The issue of drug addiction can be extended to other topics and leads us to emphasize how everyone is addicted to something and it is once again in God that we find comfort and salvation: "you got to cry without weeping/ talk without speaking/ scream without raising your voice" sings the song, and we understand how Man internalizes the problems and the needs, and even more the need for help, and only God can see into hearts and souls and understand, even without seeing the tears or hearing the words.

This part of the song can be also a prayer, the seek for God: we do not need to shout to be heard because God is always with us and within us.

We can refer also to Psalm 107, 28-30: "Then they cried out to the LORD in their trouble, and he brought them out of their distress. He stilled the storm to a whisper; the waves of the sea were hushed. They were glad when it grew calm, and he guided them to their desired haven". God rescues us by silencing the seas (the tears that we do not need to cry) and the storms (the screams that we do not need to shout) until we reach the safe and desired haven (Salvation and Heaven).

"I see seven towers/ but I only see one way out": the number seven is very important in the Bible, it symbolizes God and His perfection and completeness.

Since the story of Creation with which the Holy Book opens, we notice how the seventh day, the day of rest, carrying the divine blessing is placed as a seal to the creation itself. Later on we find seven years of famine, the seven years of plenty, the seven angels, the seven trumpets, and so on.

In a more strictly earthly field we call "seven towers of the devil" the centres of projection of the satanic influence in the world (the anti-initiation as opposed to initiation) [see for this topic The seven towers of the devil by Samir Abdulkarim Al-Hâdfî]. Even more so, therefore, the Man sees seven towers, sin and damnation, and he knows that there is only one way out: the way is God. Not surprisingly, the deadly sins are seven... We can now go back to the main theme of the song, the drug: the seven towers symbolize the ongoing struggle of Man, who, as Cain did, has turned away from God and now seeks to fill the void of his soul. This is the meaning of addiction: fill a void. But there is always a way out.

"Sweet the sin, bitter the taste in my mouth" can be compared with Revelation 10:10, "And I took the little book out of the angel's hand, and ate it up; and it was in my mouth sweet as honey: and as soon as I had eaten it, my belly was bitter".

We can also read in this a reference to the original sin: it all starts with a bite, which is even sweeter because it is forbidden, and ends then up with the expulsion and damnation that are bitter.

"You know I took the poison/ from the poison stream" is once again a reference to the original sin: the apple has been proposed by a snake, then the poison of sin comes from a poisonous animal.

The poison is also what makes bitter the sweet taste of sin.

What if we read the whole thing in reverse?

Now it is Jesus Himself who speaks, He has killed the snake (the original sin) and by shouting "it is finished" from the cross has shown the only way out after the removal of the poison (and sin) from humanity.

"Suffer the needle chill" reveals once more the parallels between the drug and the sin: the needle is the mean through which the addict injects his poison, but it is also the tooth that the snake uses to inject into us the poison of sin.

"Red Hill mining town" wants to bring out the great difficulties of the miners in carrying out their work, as well as the employment problems of this sector in the 80s. It is interesting to note that the focal point of the text is the emotional relationship, which is what is really threatened by these problems.

The emotional relationship between father and son, here named in the opening verse, can be interpreted as the relationship between God and Man. In the repeated verse "yeah you leave me holding on/ in Red Hill Town/ see lights go down, I'm.../ Hanging on/ you're all that's left to hold on to/ I'm still waiting..." we can see the Man who speaks with God: God abandons Man, leaves him to wait while the light goes down and the darkness (of evil and sin) advances; Man is conscious of the fact that he can manage to hold on despite the darkness is creeping up on the light because God is the only thing that we can hold on to.

We have to underline the verses "our love runs cold/ in the caverns of the night/ we're wounded by fear injured in dark/ I can lose myself/you I can't live without": the night has its own realm, it is in caves; this makes we think of something deep and dark that goes deep into the earth; this is a reference to hell. And it is there, in those caves, that our love becomes cold, it doesn't exists anymore. Doubt and fear hurt us, they hurt us so much that we lose ourself between them: it is the tempting sin that torture us to make us fall. Finally we find the observation: "I can not live without you". Only in God and with God there is salvation.

Later once again the observation that the Man has lost his link with God ("a link is lost/ the chain undone"), the night comes or rather we expect it well aware that it will come ("we wait all day/ for night to come/ and it comes").

There is always God to cling to in the darkness, and clinging to Him we can think higher and hope: "We scorch the earth/ set fire to the sky/ we stoop so low to reach so high" describe how much we are willing to do to reach God: we can burn the earth and set fire to the sky, we can destroy everything, we can fall down so low to be finally able to go up higher. Higher towards God.

"In God's Country" is a song that carries religious references already in the title.

Even in God's Own Country sleep comes like a drug, as a means to forget (the sins that make us unworthy of God and of His Kingdom maybe?). Even in God's Own Country we see sad eyes and crooked crosses, because it is feeling guilty for our lives and for being in a place we do not feel worthy of.

"Everyday the dreamers die/ see what's on the other side" is the realization that every day those who dream of the Kingdom of God "die", they are disillusioned because the temptations show them what's on the other hand, a world made up of sin but "easier".

In the verses "She is liberty/ and she comes to rescue me", the Holy Spirit is once again referred to as "she", a female figure who saves us from sin and temptation to prevent that the "dream", the Kingdom of God, can really die.

In "Hope, faith, her vanity/ The greatest gift is gold" we can read an almost ironic interpretation (and thus the preconception that U2 started to be ironic since Achtung Baby onwards falls) of I Corinthians 13:13: "So faith, hope, love abide, these three; but the greatest of these is love". Is therefore love the gift compared to gold? But while on the one hand this love is vanity, on the other hand it is the love that guides us, the Pure Spirit.

"I stand with the sons of Cain" refers to the story told in Genesis 4: Cain kills his brother and is sent into exile as a murderer, thus experiencing the most frightening aspect of contact with the deity ("Burned by the fire of love", where Love hurts and burns and does not forgive without having first left a mark). Cain has children in exile and one of them in particular, Jubas, is traditionally considered the ancestor of the musicians ("He was the father of all such as handle the harp and organ"). But we can interpret all this as referring to a person, here Bono, who represents every person who feels part of the children of Cain, the son of a sinner and thus sinner too. Only with the intervention of Love he may return to the Divine Light, after the payment for his sin (again, "Burned by the fire of love").

"Trip through your wires" is a song about the love for a woman who imprisons with his laces, but this imprisonment is a source of happiness. In the song, we turn to a "you" that can be interpreted as the sin, always present, as if it wanted to come to the rescue, when in fact its presence is only temptress, and we turn to "she", which is the Spirit who saves, even when it sees just in the distance a soul that is being lost.

The song ends with the same verses with which it started ("I was calling out"): first, the Man is lost in sin, trapped by it; the intervention of the Spirit frees him from those ties and makes him worthy again; sin is always there, ready to make us fall in his net and the Man falls again and again.

The verse "I was cold and you clothed me honey" is a reference to Matthew 25:35-36: "For I was hungry and you gave me food, I was thirsty and you gave me drink, a stranger and you welcomed me, naked and you clothed me". With this parallelism we return to a more standard interpretation, where the one who helps us and gives us shelter is simply and only God.

"One tree hill" is a song written in memory of Greg Carroll, the band's assistant who died in a motorcycle accident in Dublin.

"You know his blood still cries from the ground" is taken from Genesis 4:10: (once again from the story of Cain and Abel, which is taken up here after having been used in In God's Country): "The LORD said, "What have you done? Listen! Your brother's blood cries out to me from the ground".".

"I'll see you again when the stars fall from the sky..." takes up the quote which was already present in the song Fire from the album

October and refers here to Revelation 6, 12-13: "The sun is burning black... the moon is running red... the stars are falling down". There is the certainty that after death we will find us again and precisely we may see us once again in the Day of Doom.

"We run like a river to the sea" is from Ecclesiastes 1:7: "All rivers go to the sea, yet never does the sea become full. To the place where they go, the rivers keep on going". If we interpret "rivers" as a reference to every person or to their souls, we can read in these verses that although there are countless living beings and infinite souls all directed toward the same sea, to the same destination, there will be always room for other people and other souls, always and forever. Even more, the place that they reach as ultimate goal has not even seas but only rivers that continue to flow: no more death as final destination, but everlasting life.

According to the tradition of the Maori tribes, when someone died, the soul went hovering over hills and rivers to reach the sea and then it turned around to fly to Heaven.

"Exit" is a song inspired by The Night of the Hunter, a thriller movie of 1955. It sings of a man of religion that changes and becomes a murderer. Bono himself confirms this, pointing out that the change of the man is when he fails to discover and understand the mystery, discover and understand the Truth.

"Saw the hands that build can also pull down" has a double reference: we can read here Jeremiah 1:10: "See, today I appoint you over nations and kingdoms to uproot and tear down, to destroy and overthrow, to build and to plant"; we can also read here Jeremiah 31, 28: "'Just as I watched over them to uproot and tear

down, and to overthrow, destroy and bring disaster, so I will watch over them to build and to plant', declares the LORD".
The verse may be associated with "Words that build or destroy" which we find in the song Promenade. Once again it is emphasized that the same hands that build can also destroy; these can be the hands of God that give rise to all but they can so easily put an end to it all, but they can be here also the hands of someone who has always done good and is now on the other side and uses his hands of love to kill.

Chapter 7

RATTLE AND HUM (Island, 1988)

After three consecutive albums at the highest level recorded in the studio, now U2 publish an album that is a collection of live songs with the addition of nine new songs. The album celebrates the immense popularity that the band has achieved and in it, in its themes and especially in the rendering of the songs are the reasons why people love or hate U2. There is no middle ground. In this album we well notice how the band has "Americanized": we can note it in the duet with B.B. King, in the rendering of <u>I still haven't found what I'm looking for</u>, with the gospel choir that is the master. <u>Love rescue me</u> is almost a country ballad with Bob Dylan as co-author.

Not necessarily all of these influences in the album are a bad thing: this is the proof of how U2 have become a well-rounded band, able not only to bring together in one song all the topics they want to deal with, but also capable of merging in an album styles and sounds making them their own. This distinguishes them from others, because they are a mixture of music, personality and message.

"Helter Skelter" seems to be a dialogue with the devil himself.
The first strophe expresses the fall in temptations. There is an attempt to resist them ("When you get to the bottom/ you go back to the top of the slide"), then, inexorably, we surrender to the world ("And you stop and you turn/ and you go for a ride") and there we catch up, together with the temptations, the devil himself ("Then you get to the bottom/ then you see me again").
The devil describes to Man the inability to resist, no matter how great is the effort (and the instinct) to return to the top, to break away from the earthly evil to get rid of it rising towards the good (hardly, as if we are climbing on a slide that makes us fall continuously). Even when we reach the coveted top there is something that drives us to turn around and fall down, leaving the Good to get back into sin. And it is there in the background that the Evil awaits us.
In the second strophe it is the Man who speaks, accusing the devil of being him to ask for the love and to want the Man to his side. Ready to obey, the Man rushes and hopes that he can give him the answer: why do we always fall down and answer the call of evil?
"Helter Skelter" is the best expression: great is the confusion of Man. We are once again at the crossroad so recurrent in life and so often sung by U2: towards good or towards evil?

Even Milton, in his <u>Paradise Lost,</u> said, "It's better to reign in Hell than serve in Heaven", recognizing, as here, the two choices and choosing once again the evil, the most intriguing and entertaining. On the other hand, we can interpret the strophe "Do you, don't you want me to love you/ coming down fast I'm right here above you/ tell me tell me tell me the answer" as if it was the intervention of God: He asks us if we have better His love or not, He is ready to dash for us quickly to know our choice. As God, He already knows it, but He wants to be near us, watching us right in the eye when we will answer Him.

In *"Desire"* we still find the reference to drugs ("I'm like the needle, needle and spoon") as well as to other wrong things in life, whether they are weapons that spread more and more (and thus more and more wars and divisions) or whether they are false preachers who deceive people with false promises and false idols (once again the turning away from the right path and the true religion).

At the same time we find in the song also the lent itself that allows us to escape the evil, the actual "desire" to find himself in the right. In the song they still turn to the Holy Spirit as a "she", that presence to which we yearn and that we do not want to let go. Thus, at the beginning, "Lover, I'm on the street/ gonna go where the bright lights/ and the big city the meet" is a direct reference to the Holy Spirit as a lover, as the most precious thing that exists, to say that, despite being in the street, in the midst of the world and its temptations, our intention is to go to that place where the more intense light (i.e. God) will meet with the big cities (i.e. humanity).

It therefore calls for a meeting between God and Man, in Grace.

"She's a candle burning in my room" binds certain with the topic of drugs (the flame is used to dissolve the drug, and in this case finds its place also the following verse with references to the needle and the spoon) but it may also be a reference to the Holy Spirit, always present, a point of light in the darkness and destruction, the polar star indicating the right way.

Approaching the Spirit, the feeling is that of a fever that goes up and up burning, as the desire for goodness, knowledge, truth that burns in us intensifies.

"Oh sister, I can't let you go" is the key verse: after listing all that the Spirit is (power, protection, security) we come to the conclusion that we cannot do without it, and the decision is taken: "I can not let you go."

In _"Hawkmoon 269"_ are the notes of an Hammond organ (played by none other than Bob Dylan) that make up the background. It is therefore created a special atmosphere, emphasized by the biting voice of Bono. The song was inspired in part by the writer Sam Shepard, who wrote the book Hawk Moon, and it is said that it was remixed 269 times before getting to the desired result. The result is certainly spectacular, perfect, especially with the gospel choir in the final part that manages to give more strength to the whole.

Even in this song there are strong religious references.

The text is centred on the concept that God is Love, we need Love, and therefore we need God. It is also true that we all need to love one another, that is the proof and expression of the Love of

God.

The number 269 in the title can also be read as a reference in the Bible: if we search the Psalms, texts that Bono loves so much, we find in Psalm 26 the verse 9, which says: "Do not take away my soul along with sinners, my life with bloodthirsty men" (in the King James Version becomes "Gather not my soul with sinners, nor my life with bloody men"). It clearly emphasizes the concept that Bono, like anyone, feels and is a sinner (a long list of sins is present in the song), but turning to God and realizing that he needs His Love, he takes the road of salvation.

The song is a list of necessities, things closely related to each other and to which we can not give up. One thing prevails among them and on them, punctuated by the pressing repetition of the verse "I need your love". Again, the theme of the need for love, the Love of God that is for us more essential than everything else.

The repetition of the strophe "When the night has no end/ and the day yet to begin/ as the room spins around/ I need your love" is effective and explanatory: there are moments when the night seems endless, moments when the darkness around us seems to have no end; there are moments when we know that a new day has to come but it seems it does not want to rise, it seems that the light does not want to come into our lives and enlighten us so letting us get out of the darkness; the room is spinning, our mind is drunk and confused while in the dark waiting for a light late in coming. And it is in moments like these that more than ever we need the Love of the Spirit that sustains and guides us.

In the verse "Like tongues of flame" we find a biblical reference: it refers to Acts 2:3, when the apostles received the Holy Spirit:

"Then there appeared to them tongues as of fire, which parted and came to rest on each of them".

At the end of the text there are two more very significant lines: "Like faith needs a doubt" and, later, "Like lies needs the dark". The first line wishes to emphasize that faith, the true one, it is not so immediate and obvious. If there is no doubt there is no faith. We must first walk our path, ask questions, make the experiences of good and evil in order to finally find what we are looking for. And yet the doubts do not dissolve completely because faith is nourished by doubt. It is not here a matter of science, which is based on certainties. Faith is something that is born and grows within us and allows us to believe even if we are in doubt.

The second verse is opposed to this first, wanting to oppose good to evil. Faith needs the doubt and goes beyond it, in the same way the lies need the darkness they feed on. In the light we can't hide anything, in the light there is Truth; all that is temptation and lie lives in the dark side of the world and even in our own dark side.

"All along the watchtower" is a cover of a song by Bob Dylan that has also the same title. No doubt it is the most famous song among those of Dylan inspired by the Bible, and it is shot almost entirely from a chapter of the prophet Isaiah.

Historical and biblical references are here so many and on the historical and religious background should be analysed the two main characters of the Song: The Jester (the joker) and the thief.

At the beginning of the song, in the words of the jester, we see how the thrust of the song is towards finding a way out of the current state of confusion to find and reach a new dimension.

"There must be some way out of here/ said the joker to the thief./ There's too much confusion here,/ I can't get no relief": can we see in these verses the words of Christ who seeks a way out of the confusion of the world? ('Babylon' is synonymous with confusion!). The words 'juggler' or 'fool' seem to be words used to refer to Christ in thousands of Jewish anti-Christian jokes.

The verses "Businessmen they drink my wine/ Plowmen dig my earth" are a clear reference to the body (the earth) and the blood (the wine) of Christ given for the remission of sins, and "none of them know along the line/ what any of this is worth" seem to describe Christians lined up for communion without knowing really what they are going to do, without even knowing if they are worthy.

The second strophe, later repeated in the final, recalls the importance of life and the consciousness that this life is not our real destiny. The words are: "No reason to get excited/ the thief, he kindly spoke/ there are many here among us/ who think that life is but a joke/ but you and I, we've been through that/ and that is not our fate/ so let us not talk falsely now/ because the hour is getting late". It's getting late, we have so little time to understand the true meaning of life, our destiny. Among the many only a few ("you and I") have consciousness. There is no need to lie or hide the truth. Or it will be too late.

The thief who speaks to the jester is the good thief to whom Jesus will say that it will soon be with Him in Heaven; those who believe that life is just a game are the judges and the members of the Sanhedrin who mocked Jesus, saying: "You saved others, now save thyself, thou art the Son of God, the Chosen of the Lord", and the reference is also extended to the second thief who says to Jesus, "are you not the Christ? Save yourself and us then".

"Horsemen came and went" refer to the horsemen of the Apocalypse, that may also be the contrast between Dylan (and Bono) see as an artist and as a man.

"I still haven't found what I'm looking for" in the Rattle and Hum version contains the verse "He'll be your shelter from the storm", clearly taken from Psalm 55:8: "I would hurry to my place of shelter, far from the tempest and the storm". They give here a gospel version of the song that helps to intensify the effect.

"Silver and gold" is a song written for the fight against apartheid. In the song, the title certainly has a literal meaning, but it is also an expression often used in the Bible. We can find it in Deuteronomy 29:17: "You saw among them their detestable images and idols of wood and stone, of silver and gold"; it is found in Psalm 133:15: "The idols of the nations are silver and gold, made by the hands of men" and yet in Zephaniah 1:18 "Neither their silver nor their gold will be able to save them on the day of the LORD's wrath".

In the second strophe we find a possible religious reading: once again a dark and starless night is described, we speak of fallen heaven and a sun that is disappeared, chained to the ground. The end of the world has come, it is the triumph of evil over good: the sun, the symbol of light and of God, is now chained to the ground as if to say that God has changed, Its dimension is no more heavenly but earthly. The power is transferred to the devil. This thesis is supported by the verses "The warden said/ the exit is sold/ if you want a way out/ silver and gold" in which we find the reference to a guardian (undoubtedly the devil) that accepts a bribe to leave an hope. More: only paying we can hope to get out of everything. In the Divine Comedy itself it is described the path that is followed through Hell to Heaven. We meet Charon, the hell's ferryman and guardian who has to be paid to lead in the underworld, through which we will then escape to Heaven.

In the next strophe there is an invocation to Jesus. It starts with a cry that is intended to silence ("I scream at the silence"), the silence in which we are immersed when the evil has prevailed. We find once again a reference to Judas ("There's a rope around my neck") who frees and purifies himself from sin through death. The strophe ends with the real invocation to Jesus, called to account to declare Himself and to help us; there is an awareness of being someone, not something, and therefore the need of a guide to lead us in the right.

The penultimate strophe is very interesting: "chains no longer bind me/ not the shackles at my feet/ outside are the prisoners/ inside the free/ set them free" where we realize that we are not prisoners of anything, that something or someone has allowed us to dissolve the ties that bind us anchored to the negative situation in which we were.

Out are the prisoners, in those who are free: is this not a description of Heaven? In Heaven are those who are free, who have freed themselves from evil, and have chosen a righteous life; outside are all the others, the slaves of this world.

Hence the invocation "set them free": Jesus and God are the only

Ones who can save these lost souls, freeing them from their chains.

In _"Love rescue me"_ the double interpretation is really strong, on the one hand love song, on the other hand song of faith. Here we take into consideration the second interpretation.

We find immediately in the text the invocation to love (it's even in the title!). We turn to God, that is the greatest Love, and we ask for help, asking to be rescued.

In particular, the first strophe leads to the following reading: we ask God to approach us and talk to us, to support us and not let us fall. We are lost in sin and lost without love, but if He supports us we can save ourselves.

We realize that no one is an enemy to anyone, we are all the same and in the same situation. In particular, there is the realization that no one is forcing us into evil and sin, rather we let ourselves fall into temptation becoming slaves ("My own hands imprison me").

In the second strophe Bono seems to identify with any person who, like him, has been lost. The uncertainty, insecurity more properly, is reflected and we look for the confirmation of what actually we have already inside. We hope in love as a lifeline to unravel every doubt.

In the third strophe I like to read the reference to sin and to the devil himself: it is very nice the alliteration "sun - sinks - see" where the continuous repetition of the "s" sound evokes the image of the serpent, the symbol of the devil, an image that stands out ad hoc against the backdrop of lengthening shadows as the sun falls: the more we approach the darkness (evil that hides the good, the kingdom of the underworld that takes the place of a God who is gone), the more the shadows are long (the doubt that is in us increases, drawing us toward evil. This same image refers also to the idea of the shadow of evil that stretches over a world now helpless and takes possession of it).

"I'm here without a name/ in the palace of my shame" points out how in the consciousness of being in the wrong, in the shame of having abandoned God and be in sin, we are all nameless because we are all there: we are all sinners without distinction.

"Love rescue me" is the only cry.

In the fifth strophe we become aware of the power of Love, once again invoked to bring salvation. The verses "Yea though I walk through the valley of the shadow/ yet I will fear no evil/ I have cursed thy rod and staff/ They no longer comfort me..." are taken from Psalm 23: "Even though I walk in the dark valley I fear no evil; for you are at my side with your rod and your staff that give me courage". The song, in opposition to the Psalm, says that rod and staff are cursed: it is to deny religion, turn our back on God thinking that we can be self-sufficient. In the course of life, growing up, everyone lives a departure from the faith, which is then recovered thanks to God and His Love, which is the Saviour.

In verses "on the hill of the son/ I'm on the eve of a storm" there is another possible religious interpretation: the hill of the son is the site of the crucifixion of Christ. We are there and we are aware of the change: the storm that breaks out after the death of Christ is the Sky that opens to welcome Him and the world that is shaken because of the new condition of hope and salvation.

The result of the change is expressed in the last strophe, which declares defeated our past as sinners and looks towards the future.

The new world is the Heaven, we are at the gates of the new life; now the past is behind us, there are only ruins of what was once, ready to vanish in the Grace of God, the Love that saves.

"When love comes to town" is clearly a song about love, which can be once again thought more broadly as Universal Love; the song tells how wonderful is the Grace of God. We find once again the theme of the sinner who is lost but is saved by Christ, who forgives and erases all sins.

So many things are done, many mistakes are made, before Love comes to us; but we already know that when it comes we will not lose the opportunity to be better than we are because the lure of the good is too strong.

We can interpret the reference to the train as a reference to the Ascension of Christ: "all the saints will be caught up in his train", and therefore represents the desire, the hope, and almost the certainty to be in the ranks of those who will be with Christ in Heaven.

"The flame" is a reference to the Holy Spirit while in the "Great divide" we see the sin that separates us from God, but through Love everything changes, because Love can be stronger than sin ("I've seen love conquer the great divide"). Christ died on the cross because of our sins, but it is His death that bridges the gulf between Man and God because of sins.

It is very significant the strophe "I was there when they crucified my Lord/ I held the scabbard when the soldier drew his sword/ I threw the dice when they pierced his side/ but I've seen love conquer the great divide". Here a moment of the crucifixion is described and we are all present. Not only that, we are also active viewers because we take part in the crucifixion: it is also for us and for our fault that Christ died. Once again it is the Love to rejoin each division, to restore balance; it is the Love that forgives us and saves us, remedying our sins.

This part is also a biblical reference: "I was there when they crucified my Lord/ I held the scabbard when the soldier drew his sword/ I threw the dice when they pierced his side..." clearly recalls Matthew 27:35: "After they had crucified him, they divided his garments by casting lots".

"God Part II" is almost a dedication to John Lennon: the band wanted to challenge the song God by John Lennon that was surely a reference to God, but just to say that God is only a concept, He does not exist, the dream is dead and we alone stay as real things and we have to be self-sufficient. The song by U2 is instead a stress on the fact that God exists and we must believe in Him because it is His Love that we need. There is a "destructive" part in the song, which lists a series of "idols", which are sins, in which we do not believe. Temptations are accepted, but in the "constructive part" Love, that is the ability to overcome the darkness until it becomes light, comes back ("He says he's gonna kick the darkness/ 'till it bleeds daylight").

The song is a veritable hymn to God; it denies the devil and the evil that comes with him, while realizing that there can be no good without evil; that without the lies that are all around us we can not really have consciousness of truth.

"I believe in love" is the key verse, repeated at the end of each strophe: in spite of the world, we choose the Good, we choose to believe in Love, to believe in God.

In the verses "Don't believe in rock'n'roll/ can really change the world" Bono holds the thought that he has always brought with him, that the music can not change things, that the music (as a bearer of messages) can not pretend to change things. From the first song the band has written lyrics full of spirituality and with the intent to convey a clear message, but it has always been strong in their consciousness that they would never have been able to mobilize people to such an extent as to understand their message and becoming thus able to make this world a better world.

We believe only in Love, because only Love can really enter the hearts and minds and let them understand Its message.

The verses "Heard a singer on the radio late last night/ he says he's gonna kick the darkness/ 'till it bleeds daylight" can be viewed from two different perspectives: on the one hand it seems that Bono himself listens to the words of a singer, from the other hand it seems to be Bono to convey his message and the "I" can be referred to anyone who listens to him. What does not change is the message: the light must flow from the darkness. We must fight against the darkness to raise the light from it; it is the desire to defeat evil and to get from it to the good, which is the light, which is God.

Even the last strophe is to be considered for the meaning that lurks: "I feel like I'm falling/ like I'm spinning on a wheel/ It always stops beside of me/ with a presence I can feel/ I...I believe in love". It clearly expresses the feeling of being dragged into the evil, almost being forced to it; it expresses the inner confusion caused by uncertainty; it is however emphasized that finally there is something stronger that is close to us, so strong that we can perceive it, and it is Love, it is God, the only Thing that we can believe in.

"All I want is you" is once again a song that lends itself to a romantic interpretation as to a spiritual interpretation.

God may be the only thing that we really want.

"But all the promises we make/ from the cradle to the grave/ when all I want is you" testifies to the legitimacy of the spiritual interpretation: in the course of our lives there are many promises we make, some right, some wrong. Life has run its course, we charge experiences, but at the end as we are born so we die and in that very moment everything that has been disappears and all that we want is only God.

There is a strong religious reference in the verses "You'll say you'll give me/ eyes in a moon of blindness/ a river in a time of dryness/ a harbour in the tempest" which may refer to Joel 3:16, "And the Lord will be thundering from Zion, and his voice will be sounding from Jerusalem; and the heavens and the earth will be shaking: but the Lord will be a breastplate for his people and a strong place for the children of Israel". God is our refuge and our support, He alone can enable us to see the light in the darkness. Perhaps these are just promises, such as those that we humans do, but in the end it does not matter, because God is the only thing we want.

Further on in the song we find the two verses "(you want... your love) to last with me through the night" and "(you want) your love not to grow cold" that seem to be spoken by God himself rather than be turned to Him, He wants His Love, His Presence, to be always with us in the night, when we are lost in a world that takes us away from Him. He wants His Love not to shut down but to go on burning within us. Even in a world pervaded by evil and sin He wants to be with us and in us to lead us back to Love, the only thing that we really want.

Chapter 8

ACHTUNG BABY (Island, 1991)

<u>Achtung Baby</u> is going to usher in the technological breakthrough that characterizes U2 in the 90s. Even in a technological age there is place for spirituality, though now it takes on another meaning. The disc is filled with dark and even dramatic atmospheres, reflecting the crisis of art and above all the spiritual crisis that pervades the band. Compared to <u>Rattle and Hum</u> that is much more political, <u>Achtung Baby</u> is again a funny album, even behind the stronger gloomy aspect and the fun is the renewal of the band, the return to a sense of origins mixing it with the innovations of the sound, now decidedly more electric and hard.

After <u>Rattle and Hum</u>, U2 went back to 'daydreaming'. <u>Achtung Baby</u> was widely regarded as a great sound and visual reinvention of the band almost a step too far in some areas. Twenty years ago Bono described <u>Achtung Baby</u> as "the sound of four men who break down The Joshua Tree" while Jon Pareles of <u>The New York Times</u> wrote that "stripping and challenging the old formulas, U2 were given a chance to fight for all the 90s". The album won a Grammy Award for Best Rock Performance and became one of the most important records of the nineties and of U2's career.

On 9th January 1992 Elysa Gardner writes in the magazine <u>Rolling Stone</u>: "With <u>Achtung Baby</u>, U2 are once again trying to expand their musical palette, but this time their ambitions are realized. Working with producers who have worked discipline and nuances to the group's previous albums - Daniel Lanois who oversees the albums with Brian Eno and Steve Lillywhite who contribute to a number of songs - U2 propose to experiment, rather than pay homage. In this way, the band is able to draw confidently and consistently to its own devices".

Among the new elements that U2 incorporated in <u>Achtung Baby</u> we find mainly the electronic beats derived from hip-hop. The band uses these new elements in about half of the twelve songs on the album often stratifying them with the mix of heavy guitar. Bono's aim, then, is to lend his sensual tenor and his melodramatic romance to expressions that correspond to this new way of playing. This is not to say that U2 have abandoned their faith or that Bono has abandoned his quest to find what he is looking for". Mixed and melted perhaps more deeply to other topics and to the new music we always find religiosity and the search for it.

About the record, Bono himself says: "This album, <u>Achtung Baby</u>, is a new beginning and things move cyclically. I mean, there is another record that belongs to this, as well as <u>Rattle and Hum</u> belonged to <u>The Joshua Tree</u>. I know that record, I can feel it already in my head. "

Zoostation is a song inspired by the bombing that in World War II destroyed the Berlin Zoo. Many critics have analysed the song as a representation of the reinvention of the band; the first signal of the introduction into their production of a new sound and a new openness to modern technology.

Even better than the real thing is more properly a song dedicated to a woman, but in some parts there may also be spiritual interpretations.

We can think the first strophe as a prayer to God where He is asked for another chance not to disappoint Him and, this time, do not refuse Him.

"My heart is where it's always been/ my head is somewhere in between" still show uncertainty, the heel that, at some point in life, affects everyone.

The head thinks differently than the heart; the world with its temptations, with its false idols, distract our minds from those that are the true values, but the heart does not change its mind. The heart stays where it has always been, never doubting its choice and its own origins, in Good and in Truth. The heart is always with God.

The female figure to whom we address in the text can be again identified with the Holy Spirit. Even to it we ask another chance to be with Him (or "Her") to be back in Grace, to leave behind everything that with its material essence has separated us from spirituality: "We'll slide down the surface of things" is the verse that underlines this. It's also worth noting the last strophe of the song: "We are free to fly the crimson sky/ the sun won't melt our wings tonight/ Oh now... here she comes/ take me higher". The image of the red sky is back in these verses, the sky of the changing. We are free to fly in it, even if most often this sky is a sign of the Apocalypse and we know it. In any case, the sun (here no longer God but evil) can not make us fall to the ground because the Holy Spirit is always with us and it is the means by which we can climb higher, higher and higher, again over Evil and towards God.

One will become perhaps the most famous song of the group, a track that is both evocative and spiritual and deals with love as universal love. The interpretation so full of devotion given by Bono nears and compares it with a prayer.

The most obvious interpretation sees the text simply as a difficult love affair: two people who are unable to maintain a stable relationship for constant bickering and mutual wounds. An interview with The Edge by <u>Q Magazine</u> seems to support this theory. Some interpretations see in <u>One</u> uniqueness in a spiritual sense, others tend to associate the text to German reunification relating with the period spent by the band in Germany. Bono describes the theme of the song as follows: "This is a song about being together, but not like the old hippie idea "we all live together". This is, in fact, the opposite. He is saying that we are one, but we are not the same thing. He is not saying that we want to be together for a long time, but we have to be together for a long time in this world to survive. This reminds us that we have no choice".

Analysing the three videos that the band has created for this song, we find the following interpretations:

- The first, directed by Anton Corbijn in Berlin sees Bono confess to his father that he has been affected by HIV: One would therefore be a gay son.

- The second offers a panorama of lush flowers and buffaloes, on which stands a rain of cards with the word One written on several languages. We may note that the cover depicts a work by David Wojnarowicz, an American painter known to be homosexual, and that the buffaloes come from one of his works too.

- The third shows Bono sitting in a bar while drinking beer and smoking a cigar. The angles at which it was taken, added to soft light, gave rise to a criticism because we can see in the video a kind of affinity with Heineken advertising. In any case, it makes a clear idea of a relationship that has come to an end.

In my opinion we can add also a religious interpretation, in which we are all "one" with God.

The song can be read as a dialogue with God, a statement addressed to Man. If things go wrong we blame God as the first cause, and this seems to be the shortest way not to ask questions, to really understand where and how we are wrong because things are not going as they should.

"One love/ one life/ when it's one need/ in the night" is once more the Love of God: God Himself tells us that one is the Love that is also life (the only life) and it is the only need in the night (here again sin): it is only with God's Love that we leave the sinful condition to return to the light.

The song then continues "one love/ we get to share it/ leaves you baby if you/ do not care for it" to reaffirm how one and universal is love, we must share it not only with each other, but also and especially with God that gives it to us. If we look the other way and we turn the other side then Love abandons us and with it God too. We find then ourselves in a world that is only sin and neglect. Then is God to ask us if we were disappointed or if He has "wronged", it is with resentment that He says "you act like you never had love/ and you want me to go without": to Him we act as if He had never given us Love, as if he had abandoned us to our fate, and for that, almost out of spite, we also want Him to feel the same, we deny Him our love and we try to let Him in His Infinite.

"We are one, but we're not the same" is an important line: it emphasizes how we are one with God, how we are all united together in His Love, but by no means we are the same thing: God is infinite as infinite is also His Love, we can not even think of trying to substitute for It.

This concept can be revised in other words in the verses "Have you come here for forgiveness/ have you come to raise the dead/ have you come here to play Jesus/ to the lepers in your head". It is almost as if we wanted to present ourselves before God to show Him that we are like Him, we are enough for forgiveness, we are enough to bring back to life those who are no more (or, more broadly, to bring back to Good all those who are lost in sin); we are preachers as it had been Jesus, and we hope that this is enough to defeat and drive out our demons.

"We hurt each other/ then we do it again" well expresse the conflictual relationship between God and Man: it is a relationship of continuous love and hate. God hurts us because it is with pain and suffering that He tests our strength and our faith. On the other side we hurt God by continuously denying Him and with the constant yield to temptation. Then the conflict disappears, Love envelops all and brings us together, at least until we resume again to hurt ourselves.

The verses that follow seem to be the answer of Man, "you say/ love is a temple/ love the higher law// you ask me to enter/ but then you make me crawl/ and I can't be holding on/ to what you got/ when all you got is hurt". You, God, You say that Love is a temple, that Love is the highest of the laws; You, God, that ask me to enter the Temple, to join You in Your Love, but then I find myself crawling, humble sinner, unworthy of the place where I am. Thus, almost abandoned, it is impossible to remain in harmony with God for all that He gives us is pain and suffering, He only tests our faith with suffering.

Eventually, however, we draw just one conclusion: we are One Love, we need each other because without God there is no Man and without Man there can be no God. Although not the same, we are ONE.

*Until the end of the world* is a song commissioned by Wim Wenders for the soundtrack of the homonymous film.
With the title the song already evokes an image of the religious tradition, the end of the world. Throughout the song and, more particularly, in the end of it, we can connect the "end of the world"

with its biblical significance.

The dark rock is a background to the dialogue between Jesus and Judas, a dialogue which is lowered into an almost diabolical atmosphere. The song expresses Judah's perspective: is there hope for him or not? The betrayal was part of God's plan, it is Judas who has to bear the responsibility and the weight of this action. In this sense, the song speaks also of us: we are all sinners, so if Jesus died because of the sins of the world, we too are responsible and we have to carry the weight of our responsibility.

The first strophe can be read as a reference to the Last Supper: "Last time we met was a low-lit room/.../ we were as close together as a bride and groom/ we ate the food, we drank the wine/ everybody having a good time/ except you/ you were talking about the end of the world" but we can also read in it the relationship between God and the Church: in Ephesians Paul speaks of the Church considering it as the wife of Christ, the bridegroom.

In the passage can be emphasized the reference to the bread and wine, the rite of Communion, accomplished by Christ at the Last Supper. In the room all were happy to sit at the table with Christ, but He spoke of His death and of the end of the world (the world as we knew it).

In the second strophe we find the reference to Judas's betrayal: "I took the money". It is Judas himself who speaks, he refers the doubts and uncertainties, likens himself to a whore because he has not lived up to its values and has sold himself to the highest bidder.

"I kissed your lips and broke your heart" is the kiss of Judas the traitor who disappoints in full the expectations and the confidence of his Master. And He speaks again of the end of the world, knowing the fate of Man.

The last strophe is a discourse of Judah that can be identified here with anyone since we are all human and sinners: the pain can not be defeated, rather it is the pain that draws us deeper and deeper. The pain is the sin that clings to us in its web. It is at the same time regret and joy, because on one hand we repent for the mistakes we made but on the other hand this constant escape from the right values gives us joy. Evil is funnier than Good.

At the end we reach out to the Saviour (Judas towards that God betrayed by him, and thus destroyed; we towards that God that we deny with our sins but to Whom we finally turn to try to be back in the right).

With "waves of regret" there is almost a reference to Confession: Judas realizes the consequences of his actions and regrets it. He accepts Christ anew in himself.

Finally, an observation: "You said you'd wait/ 'til the end of the world" is the promise that Christ had made: until the end of the days He would have waited for us, repentant sinners, in order to rise us to a new life with Him, in the Glory of the Father.

Even in this song can be traced some biblical references:

"We ate the food, we drank the wine... I took the money, I spiked your drink... In the garden I was playing the tart, I kissed your lips and broke your heart" refers to Judas and Jesus in 26 Matthew 14:15 ("Then one of the twelve, who was named Judas Iscariot, went to the chief priests and said, What will you give me, if I give him up to you? And the price was fixed at thirty bits of silver".);

26 26:28 ("And when they were taking food, Jesus took bread and, after blessing it, he gave the broken bread to the disciples and said, Take it; this is my body. And he took a cup and, having given praise, he gave it to them, saying, Take of it, all of you, for this is my blood of the testament, which is given for men for the forgiveness of sins".), 26 47:49 ("And while he was still talking, Judas, one of the twelve, came, and with him a band armed with swords and sticks, from the chief priests and those in authority over the people. Now the false one had given them a sign saying, The one to whom I give a kiss, that is he: take him. And straight away he came to Jesus and said, Master! and the gave him a kiss".).

"Who's gonna ride your wild horses" seems to be the reaction of Jesus to Judas' betrayal, treated in the song Until the end of the world. It is a song of forgiveness, and it is also evident by comparing the atmosphere and the tone of the voice of the two songs: so dark and distressing the previous one, so more open and light in this second one..

I interpret this song as a dedication to the Holy Spirit, which once again is referred to as a "she". In the first verse it is called "dangerous" because "honest": honesty is indeed a double edged sword. It also underlines the ambiguity of the Holy Spirit, at once a tempter to test the robustness of our faith and a means of salvation.

It can be seen how, when the Spirit is no more there, when we have left It to go to forsake us to sin, our heart is empty and at the mercy of all those spirits who want to control it, at the mercy of sins and temptations.

The second strophe is still referred to the Holy Spirit, but now the Spirit is the divine message: the message is dangerous because the message It brings is too big for us and scares us; It is so far away because when It reveals God to us It leaves us apart since we do become worthy to come to Him.

"Hallelujah, heavens white rose/ the doors you open/ I just can't close" is the praise to Heaven, symbolized by the colours of Grace and Purity. Only the Holy Spirit can open Its doors and we, even in our earthly condition of sinners, are unable to close Them. At the end of everything is God who triumphs.

In the next strophe Bono seems to ask the Holy Spirit not to turn to look, not to consider what we have been before welcoming Him and being back in the right. The past is past and we hope it remains so to be able to enjoy a new life in God.

"Well you left my heart empty as a vacant lot/ for any spirit to haunt" is Luke 11:24-26: "When the unclean spirit has gone out of a person, it passes through waterless places seeking rest, and finding none it says, "I will return to my house from which I came". And when it comes, it finds the house swept and put in order. Then it goes and brings seven other spirits more evil than itself, and they enter and dwell there. And the last state of that person is worst than the first".

"So cruel" is more properly a love song focused particularly on the difficulties that may present a relationship but the song leaves open once again the interpretation of Love seen as God's Love. The relationship described becomes the relationship between Man and God.

We have exceeded the limit that separates good from evil, trying to stay afloat to see the other fall: it is the Man who abandons himself to sin and the God that he denied is left to decay; it is also God who realizes that the Man is now hopelessly lost, but God tries to stay present to see him sink into evil.

God has disappeared from the view of Man as Man is now out of the sphere of God's influence. We find here the observation that Man has tried to give God what He wanted, but it was not enough. Thus they move away from each other. But we can here also observe that God has always been close to Man trying to give him everything he needed, but the Man always wants more, so the Man is plunged into the abyss of demons, turning away from God. "The man who loves you, you hate the most" points out the futility of love that we are trying to express, because, as is often the case, the more we have the less we give; he who spends himself to do good is not considered. He who gives more love receives in return only hate, perhaps because it is assumed that he will always be there and we want to get out of the sphere of influence of a love so great to be able to try something different.

More concerning is the interpretation which sees in the man who has loved us Christ Himself. He Who has loved us more than anyone else is repaid with hatred: He was crucified for having preached Love.

Later in the text we find the reference to the "dove of God" ("God's only dove"), a symbol of peace and purity, and the reference to the angel ("screams like an angel for your love"). It stresses the need for love and the angels, already in Grace, yearn for this Love too. This need is underlined at the end of the strophe, with the verse "you need her like a drug": still we find the reference to the Holy Spirit, the "she" who embodies the Love of God.

It is very interesting the line "head in heaven, fingers in the mire" where we can well see the dichotomy Good/ Evil; salvation/ sin: the head is in Heaven, the fingers are in the mud. There is the attachment of the body to all that is earthly and material and leads to sin, but the spirit turns to higher goals and tends to Heaven, the Good.

"Between the horses of love and lust we are trampled underfoot" is in the Book of Kings 2, 9:33 (The Death of Jezebel): "Throw her down!" Jehu said. So they threw her down, and some of her blood spattered the wall and the horses as they trampled her underfoot".

It should however be analysed into a broader context: "The night is bleeding like a cut/ between the horses of love and lust/ we are trampled underfoot". It leads us once again to the concept of sin that overcomes the Man, through the symbolism of the end of the world and of the evil that advances: the sky is torn and is bleeding; a demon rises from the darkness, evoked by the sound of horses' hooves. The tradition has that the the devil's advance is a clatter of hooves!

The horses also symbolize the gap between Good and Evil: they are Love and Lust, the Spiritual against the Material. Which one have we to choose? And under the weight of this choice we end up crushed. The fighting of Man is also revealed in the last verses of the song: "to stay with you I'd be a fool" is the rejection of God and of His Love: only a fool would accept It.

But finally we go back to the origin: there is cruelty in God's Love because It is not easy to reach and to be worthy of, but the word "sweetheart" is the sense of all: how difficult it is, we will never be able to say no to Love.

"The fly" is a song that refers to the end of the world, at least of the world as we know it, the world of the true values being replaced by the modern world of consumerism.

The description of the end of the world, with the stars falling from the sky, the star that burns, is part of the Apocalypse, as well as the reference to the one that lies, the Antichrist, the bearer of the wrong values.

The first three strophes speak of the Apocalypse, the darkness that envelops everything, eclipsing the sun too. Once again we see the world as immersed in sin and the light, God, disappears behind this blanket of evil. Man denies God getting away from Him, captured by the false promises of sin.

In the verse "You know I don't see you when she walks in the room" there is still the identification of the Holy Spirit with a female figure. She comes to us, but in reality we can not see who is behind her: the Holy Spirit is God, but we can only see the First continuing to ignore the Second.

The verses "a man will beg/ a man will crawl/ on the sheer face of love" describe the human condition: we are conscious of Love and of Its meaning, but it is difficult to reach the goal. We are forced to beg and pray and crawl to be able to yearn to it.

In the verses "It's no secret that a conscience/ can sometimes be a pest" returns the image of a Man torn between good and evil: to have a conscience can be a nuisance because it makes us think. We are always tempted and fall into sin, but our conscience will not let us rest easy in the condition of sinners and makes us think and makes us realize that we are not in the right.

In the refrain "A man will rise/ a man will fall/ from the sheer face of love" the uncertainty of the human condition is reiterated: Love lifts us up but at the same time It sinks us because although we strive to Love It seems so big and unattainable that we allow ourselves to fall into what is earthly and material.

Why not read in the two described cases the reference to Christ and Lucifer? The first is the One that has arisen from Love and Who leads through It to salvation; the second is Lucifer, who fell from the Love and the Grace to have his own kingdom, the Evil.

The ambivalence that I have just analysed is also found in the verses "Love we shine like a burning star/ We're falling from the sky tonight" in which we find once again God against the Devil, Good versus Evil. On the one hand we are stars that burn in the sky, we are in the right, we are in God; on the other hand we are falling stars, as Lucifer is a fallen angel, and we are therefore on the wrong side. More specifically these verses are found in Luke 10:18: "Jesus said to them, "I saw Satan fall like lightning from the sky"."

In the last strophe returns the theme of the betrayal of Judas and the reference to the call to God: "The universe exploded 'cause of one man's lie" is nothing more than the betrayal of Judas, the lie that causes a total upheaval of things.

"Look, I gotta go, yeah I'm running outta change" is the call, a recurring theme in the songs by U2. The coins end up, the communication is lost, we can do nothing but go away and come back to our lives as Men.

"Mysterious ways" can be read as the description of a relationship between God and Man. We talk about living underground, which is a clear reference to life without the presence of God, a life totally unsatisfactory.

God moves in mysterious ways, we can neither see nor know where He is and how He affects our lives, how He will manifest His presence. As in other cases, even here "she" can be interpreted as referring to the Holy Spirit. The song becomes a dedication to the Holy Spirit and hides the reference to the relationship between John the Baptist and the Holy Spirit.

In the first strophe there is an exhortation to let in this figure in our lives, even if it is only pale light, imperceptible presence.

In the verses "you've been living underground/.../ you've been running away/ from what you don't understand/ love" the description of the human condition: we get away from what we do not understand because it is scary, we live underground (metaphor for hell) because it is easier to understand Evil rather than Good. And the Good is Love.

"She'll be there when you hit the ground", confirms that the Holy Spirit will be with us when we will hit the ground, that is when we will be overcome by temptation.

The verse "She moves in mysterious ways" reminds us to how many and mysterious are the ways and means in which and for which the Spirit acts and intervenes in our lives.

Still we find "Let her talk about the things you can't explain" that emphasizes how small and powerless we are in comparison with infinity, that is God: there are so many things that we can not explain and understand and only thanks to the intervention of the Spirit they may seem closer and clearer to us.

The Spirit who speaks of "things you can't explain" can also be found in Romans 8:26: "Likewise the Spirit also helpeth our infirmities: for we know not what we should pray for as we ought: but the Spirit itself maketh intercession for us with groanings which cannot be uttered.". In addition, Bono himself reveals that at the end of the song he deals with the Spirit Itself.

The verse "If you want to kiss the sky better learn how to kneel" is at a first interpretation, a line of highly erotic content. Analysed in the background of a religious interpretation it is the mere reference to prayer (you must kneel to pray), but also the necessary condition to attain Heaven. They are not only key verses of the song but, in my opinion, the perfect description of what is the faith: we must kneel, begging for forgiveness and leaving the temptations of the world (with the mysterious help of the Holy Spirit), to aspire to the highest level, to God. The more we are down, the more we can hope to climb; the more we are willing to bow, the more we can hope to get to Heaven. Hence the exhortation "kneel!" ("On your knees boy"), which comes from Bono who still asks us to look beyond what is around us, but comes also from the Holy Spirit.

In the last strophe we find a further confirmation that this is a song dedicated to the Holy Spirit: the verses literally sing "Spirit moves in mysterious ways/ she moves with it/ lift my days, light up my nights" and confirm how the Spirit knows how to manifest in ways that are varied and mysterious, how She can be present in our lives at all times, in the good as in the evil, raising the days in the divine light and illuminating our nights to save us from the darkness.

A strictly biblical reading leads us to Mark 6:17-29 where we find the story of Salome. Oscar Wilde himself wrote about this topic and many elements of the song can be linked to his work: see for example the moon, Johnny, the living underground, the line "running away from what you do not understand," the belly dance and the title too.

"Tryin' to throw your arms around the world" may indicate an attempt to conquer a woman, but also an attempt to conquer God. An attempt to be almost like Him, to embrace everything to have it all. But we are not God, and everything will take us away from Him; only the deserving and those who do not aspire to be God can reach Him. This is expressed in the verses "He took an open top Beetle/ through the eye of a needle" that are a clear reference to Luke 18:24-25: "Jesus looked at him now sad and said, "How hard it is for those who have wealth to enter the kingdom of God! For it is easier for a camel to pass through the eye of a needle than for a rich person to enter the kingdom of God."".

"Ultraviolet (Light my way)" is again a song that deals with Love and His strength.

Man is often weak and in need of support, and once again it is the Love that sustains him.

"The day is as dark as the night is long" describes how the night (the Evil) also affects the day (the Good): the more the first one is longer, the more the other one approaches almost to merge into it. Metaphorically speaking, the more evil affects us becoming more and more the master of our lives, the more the light that was in our life dies, and so we turn away from the Good.

Then there is the invocation to Love: "I'm in the black, can't see or be seen// baby... light my way". Man is plunged in the darkness of evil, he can not see or be seen, he can not be saved. There remains only the possibility of invoking God's Love to light the way, to bring light into the darkness of sin, to bring the Good where there is now only the Evil.

In _"Acrobat"_ we see expressed the uncertainty of the Faith, the Man who wavers in his human and religious journey.

In the first verses there is the willing to put on guard in front of everything that we, more or less unconsciously, face: "don't believe what you hear/ don't believe what you see/ if you just close your eyes/ you can feel the enemy" is the exhortation to look around and do not take everything that we face and everything we are told as gospel.

We are not puppets that depend on someone to get a life, we are thinking beings and we must be able to distinguish and decide.

Only if we are able to stop for a moment and realize everything that surrounds us we can really understand that we are in the evil and that we are far from the correct path.

The uncertainty is expressed in its higher tones with the third strophe. We find the lines "if there was one I could believe in/ I'd break bread and wine/ if there was a church I could receive in/ 'cause I need it now" which express the need to believe in someone (or something); the need to be one with God in a church that we can accept as our own and at the same time can accept us. The church is not meant as a building, but as a communion of people looking in the same direction and yearning for their highest goal.

The question is: is there really someone to believe in?

The reference to the rite of Communion is intended to indicate the Christian God and the desire to be part of a community, in Him and with Him.

Love is blindness closes the album by bringing a little bit of peace. The apparent tranquillity, however, is full of fear and gloom: Bono reaches the awareness that love is blind. From here comes therefore a parallel between the love and the looming sense of death.

The first lines say "Love is blindness/ I don't want to see/ won't you wrap the night/ around me", reiterating that Love is to be blind, we do not even want to look because the darkness surrounds us and if we want to escape from it our only hope is Love.

But Love is to be blind, then we should not even try to look to understand.

The song goes on saying how in the little things of every day we perceive the presence of love and it is through love that we can keep ties firm.

Love is compared to a danger, because so great is Its power that it almost instil fear. Do not look, do not try to understand the meaning, to accept It and receive It in Its infinite being is enough. Because Love is to be blind.

Chapter 9

ZOOROPA (Island, 1993)

Zooropa is one of the less appreciated albums of the band. The atmosphere and style now come off significantly from their earlier work: they try to keep pace with the times turning more towards the electronic and commercial. The album ranges from more involved songs and more idiotic songs, through all the styles and influences; at the height of popularity U2 can afford everything.

Continuing where <u>Achtung Baby</u> left off, <u>Zooropa</u> submits deeply in that new love that U2 feel for experimental music and discotheques. It can be said that the initial track still creates a bridge between those who are new inspirations and those who were hymns in <u>The Joshua Tree</u>, while the rest of the album is definitely more daring and seems even to wander aimlessly.

Nevertheless, even in <u>Zooropa</u> we can trace the themes that recurred already in the previous albums, including the religious theme.

In *"Lemon"* we see a woman dressed in lemon yellow: she is the imagination, she is Heaven and the final destination. We note the reference in the verses "And when you're dry/ She draws her water from the stone" that are a recovery of Numbers 20:8: "[God said to Moses] "Take this staff and assemble thee community, you and your brother Aaron, and in their presence order the rock to yield its waters. From the rock you shall bring forth water for the community and their livestock to drink"."".

In the song is expressed the dichotomy light (i.e. Heaven and Spirit) versus the material and earthly being. "You" always refers to the Spirit, which is light and at the same time transparent in the light: we can not see it.

So many have consumed the entire life looking for the woman dressed in lemon yellow, but in reality she comes when she is not expected... creativity comes from the deepest darkness and allows us to rise. In the same way life comes from death.

With the lines of the second strophe is once again expressed the uncertainty of the human condition, the moment of doubt that leads to renounce to faith: "And I feel/ like I'm slowly slipping under/ And I feel/ like I'm holding onto nothing" is nothing more than a description of how Man feels attracted to all that is material and earthly around him, and in an attempt to resist he clings to something that suddenly does not feel anymore a grip.

Therefore he abandons himself to sin.

The third strophe sings "she wore lemon/ to colour in the cold gray night/ she had heaven/ and she held on so tight" and describes the Holy Spirit Itself: the Spirit is light (here in the metaphor of lemon yellow) and as such can illuminate the dark night of sin. It is the Spirit which has Heaven in It because the Spirit is part of It, and keeps It because immune from the temptations and sins, to bring It to the Man.

Further on, with the strophe "and I feel/ like I'm drifting from the shore/ and I feel/ like I'm swimming out to her" we have the opposition and almost the answer to what has been expressed in the second strophe. Here the Man does not indulge in sin anymore because he has nothing to cling to, but after another moment of uncertainty that makes him falter and away from the "beach", from his destination, he finds himself finally to swim to the Spirit, the beacon in the night. Again, it is thanks to the intervention of the Holy Spirit that doubt is resolved, and the Man finds God.

The concept is reiterated in the verses sung in falsetto: "You're gonna meet her there/ she's your destination/ there's no sleeping there/ she's imagination/ Lemon/ she had heaven/ she wore lemon". Again here the Spirit is indicated as our destination, the Spirit is like a dream, something ethereal and perhaps unattainable, but it is Heaven and the Light that can guide us.

Bono wrote this song thinking about the last time when his mother was alive. Through a movie he can remember these moments, and in this sense, he sings the possibility of using films as a means to keep memories alive.

As concerns the video, it can be seen how specific symbols appear against the background : a pendulum that moves, a clock that emits its ticking, dollars that come from the sky, scientific objects (such as DNA or satellites) and a cross. These symbols represent all Man's attempt to save time, either through technology or money and also by using religion. In the video finally appears Bono in the guise of Mr. "The Fly" and "MacPhisto", the first symbols of the new consumerism compared to the old values of religion.

"Stay (faraway, so close)" can be seen as a song that tells the story of an angel in love with a human, the contact is tried to be kept but it is impossible the former being unreal, not physically present, and the second real. It is the contrast between the real world and what instead is over reality. At the end of the song the angel becomes human, we find "hits the ground", the angel falls heavily to the ground, not because it gets physicality but because it enters the real world, it is in the world. We can read the song also as the attempt to help those who can not or will not be helped: we are there, but we are like angels, invisible. We focus on action, but in the end we are only mortals (like angels hitting the ground).

In the song we still speak of the relationship between Man, Good and Evil, and it seems at times that God Himself talks to Man.

In the first strophe stand the lines "You say when he hits you, you don't mind/ because when he hurts you, you feel alive" which refer to the concept that we accept the evil so easily because it is funnier. Sure, it leaves its mark when it hits, but it does not matter: we pretend not to feel it just because the pain that causes us becomes the stimulus of a life otherwise monotonous.

Evil is also the protagonist of the second strophe and we find this in the verses "you stumble out of a hole in the ground / a vampire or a victim/ it depends on who's around". The hole in the ground is a metaphor for Hell. We can come out as victims of the tempting sin but also as perpetrators of evil. It depends on the circumstance and convenience. Similarly, we can read here the reference to Lucifer, who comes out of his underground kingdom to bring the evil in the world: he is the bearer of temptation and sin, but he is also a victim of his own evil that caused his fall from Heaven.

In the third and fourth strophe God speaks to us directly:

and if you look, you look through me	it is through God's eyes that we see and understand
and when you talk, you talk at me	we always speak with God
and when I touch you, you don't feel anything	when God touches us with His Grace we do not feel Him because He is already in us
If I could stay then the night would give you up	God asks us to let Him be with us, not drive Him out, as it is by His presence that night, and the evil, will not get the better of us.

Still, further on, He tells us "if you shout, I'll only hear you" to make us understand that in times of need, when we find ourselves screaming because abandoned and sinners, the only one who will hear our cries will be God, always in us and with us.

Even in this song we find a biblical reference: "Stay with the demons you drowned" is in Matt 9:31-32: "The demons pleaded with [Jesus], "If you drive us out, send us into the herd of swine". And he said to them: "Go then!" They came out and entered the swine, and the whole herd rushed down the steep bank into the sea where they drowned".

The demons are drowned, the spirits found, and with the triumph of the day on the night a single noise cuts the silence: it is the sound of an angel that touches the ground. The interpretation that can be given to the figure of the angel is double: it may be a reference to Lucifer, the fallen angel, who hurled from Heaven sinks into the bowels of the earth (thus emphasizing the triumph of good over evil), but can be also the angel that each of us has beside, which runs from Heaven to Earth by entering with clamour in our lives to support us in the choices and difficulties.

"Daddy's gonna pay for your crashed car" just makes me think of the parallel father/ God. Here God is more familiarly called "Father", a more daily and intimate term, which suggests a less rigorous and more affective relationship.

Dad (God) is always at our side ready for any eventuality: He comforts us in our solitude (which is the confusion that captures the Man in the world), He fulfils our desires, He takes upon Himself the responsibility for our mistakes, forgiving and making up for them.

The "crashed car" is both the single trouble and all human life wasted in sin and in the material.

In the third strophe this concept is much stronger:

you've got a head full of traffic	is the confusion that pervades the Man
you cry for mama and daddy is right along	is the continuous search for support in something other, while God is ready to run for us
he gives you the keys to a flamin' car	is according to me a reference to Heaven: only God can have the keys and Heaven is like a new car; a new life is replacing our lives as sinners
Daddy' ll hold your hand right up to the end	simply tells us that God will be with us until the end and thus this line sums up the whole meaning of the song

"Some days are better than others" is a song that tells how the days are not all the same.

Read in religious terms it can be said that a distinction is made between those days in which we feel more attracted to the earthly things and lost in them and those days in which we tend to God.

As an example I can quote the lines "Some days it all adds up/ and what you got is not enough" that express the need to have more and more, to take refuge in what is earthly and in consumerism to have more and more.

In contrast we find the verse "some days you're thankful for what you got" that tells us how there are days in which we do not need to look for something else but we are just grateful for what we have. These are the days that we live closer to God.

In verses "Some days you feel like a bit of a baby/ looking for Jesus and His mother" we can read the bewilderment of Man: there are days when we do not know what to do, which side to take. We feel children once again because children still have the courage to break away from the world and seek God, seek solace and support in something higher.

The refrain is to be quoted: "some days you hear a voice/ taking you to another place/ some days are better than others". It still tells us how God's presence is always strong and active in our lives: His is the voice that we hear resound and that is able to take us somewhere else, away from the material world and higher, in the Spirit.

And these are the best days.

"The first time" gives the impression of being a simple and pure poetic moment in the midst of chaos. It tells of an interior disorientation with religious images similar to the prodigal son's wandering in the parable that best describes the God of Christians (Luke 15, 11-32): "He gave me the keys to his kingdom to come." It tells of forgiveness: "For the first time I feel love" is the love that we feel by receiving forgiveness.

Edge says: "I have always considered that text next to the themes of our first album, almost as <u>I will follow</u>. There is this sense of unconditional love, with the response that is almost the opposite of what you might imagine: run away instead of run towards it. Although sometimes it is the right answer".

Bono said: "It's about losing faith. I have not lost my faith but I feel very sympathetic to those who have the courage not to believe. I have seen many people around me who have had bad experiences with religion, so bad that they do not feel like going back to it anymore, and it's a shame".

In the song terms as "lover" and "brother" are used, terms that identify Jesus at best.

In the first two strophes there is a reference to the Holy Spirit, the perfect lover who teaches us to sing, and, more specifically, teaches us those songs that are praises to God. The colours that it shows us are the colours of the Good and the Grace, The colours of the true life. Colours are positive when we are immersed in the darkness of sin and the effect is to make us feel love for the first time and it is the Love of God.

The two following strophes speak of Christ: He is the brother we always have at our side, ready to rise us again when the sin sinks us winning our souls. It still makes us feel love.

Finally God Himself is mentioned, the rich man (wealthy because Almighty). He and He alone can give us the keys to the "kingdom to come", "the Heaven". "Gave me the keys to His Kingdom coming" is a reprise of Matthew 16:19: "[Jesus said to Peter] "I will give you the keys to the kingdom of heaven. Whatever you bind on earth shall be bound in heaven; and whatever you loose on earth shall be loosed on heaven".".

I interpret the gold cup ("the cup of gold") as a reference to the Grail, the cup of the Last Supper. Through it Christ has detached from all that is earthly, but in doing so has washed away our sins. God offers us the cup to be able to forgive us once again; at the same time He leaves us the freedom to choose our life: we have many doors in front of us and we have to decide which one to open.

The verses "He said "I have many mansions/ and there are many rooms to see"" are a reference to John 14:2, "In my Father's house are many mansions: if it were not so, I would have told you. I go to prepare a place for you".

Almost to avoid the choice, not to face a tortuous path, the Man chooses to run away and does this almost in secret, leaving the back, and then by choosing that way he comes back in sin and stays there.

It may be pointed out as in the figure of Bono, who as always represents every single person, we may find the figures of both Judah and Peter: the first leaves by the back door ("I left by the back door"), turns away from God with his betrayal, almost slinking away; the second throws the keys and turns away from God ("I trew away the keys", after he had been offered). In any case, there is, in short, the loss of God's Grace and the wanting to follow one own way on their own. The tone of the song is thus really sad. At the end there are again joy and hope: "For the first time I feel love" is the return to God and to His Love.

"The wanderer", sung with Johnny Cash, is a song about redemption, about a man who looks for himself and looks for

God in the midst of sin. So the streets are paved with gold because material things attract, but the city is soulless because sin has had the upper hand. The Man tries everything ("To taste and to touch and to feel as much as a man can") before realizing that the only useful thing is God and return to Him ("before he repents") and be back to Love.

There are strong religious references in the song: "Through streets paved with gold" comes from Revelation 21:21: "The twelve gates were twelve pearls, each gate of a single pearl. The great street of the city was of pure gold, like transparent glass".

"Who would sit at his Father's right hand" is from Matthew 26:64: ""Yes, it is as you say", Jesus replied. "But I say to all of you: In the future you will see the Son of Man sitting at the right hand of the Mighty One and coming on the clouds of heaven".".

As Bono himself confirms, another possible title for this piece is "The Preacher" because while not exactly mirroring the text the spirit of the entire song refers to the entire Book of Ecclesiastes which is also sometimes called "The Preacher". To confirm this it's enough to underline the already mentioned lines "I went out there in search of experience/ to taste and to touch and to feel as much as a man can before he repents" which is a clear revival of Ecclesiastes 11:9: "Rejoice, o young man, while you are young, and let your heart be glad in the days of your youth. Follow the ways of your heart, the vision of your eyes; yet understand as regards all this God will bring you to judgement".

The lines "I went with nothing/ nothing but the thought of you/ I went wandering" emphasize that in the wanderings of Man in a world of temptations God is always at his side. Here Man is alone but God is with him in thought, and the Man does not stop, continues in his travels.

In the following strophe is yet described a world marked out by evil and sin, a world where the rules are reversed. We have to notice the lines "they say they want the kingdom/ but they don't want God in it" in which we see the reversal of the concept: it is easier wishing for God than for His Kingdom, because God is a support in life while His Kingdom is still tied to the concept of death. Here, however, the Man wants the Kingdom of God, which is Power and Eternity, but does not want God. God is useless: if in evil and sin we have already everything, we do not need a God Who wants to change our lives, we just need the Kingdom to enjoy forever what we have.

In the repetition of the chorus there is a change: now the man does not go out wandering with the thought of God any more but comes out with the intent to seek God in his wanderings. There is a gradual move away from the earthly world to move towards the right and the spiritual.

In the last strophe all the concepts that through the wandering lead to God are explained: the wandering of Man is designed to get experience, to touch what is the world and try everything before coming to repentance and return to God.

After gaining experience there comes the time of seeking God: "I went out searching/ looking for one good man/ a spirit who would not bend or break/ who would sit at his Father's right hand". Actually it is about the search of Christ, the Good Man and the Tough Spirit that brought the message and had the courage to die for that message and for us. And now He sits at the right hand of the Father.

The image of a man who goes to seek for God with the Bible and the gun is really meaningful: it is once again the image of a man torn between Good and Evil, which seeks the Good but can not leave behind the Evil. Now the road is taken and we get to say: "Jesus, don't you wait up/ Jesus I'll be home soon" because we are already aware of the fact that our road will take us back home soon, with Christ, in God.

We come thus to the last observation: "I left with nothing/ but the thought you'd be there too// I left with nothing/ nothing but the thought of you": we do not need anything in our wandering, just the thought of God and the certainty that He is there and we will find Him at the end of our wanderings.

Zooropa can be divided into two parts: the first section deals with the new values and the new world that surrounds us and is more properly "consumerist" while then, as the songs follow each other, there is a progressive awareness of the situation and of the need to seek God. This song is the highlight of this second part.

The rendering of the tools that should be used for the search is really beautiful: "I went out walking/ with a Bible and a gun". The Man walks the world, in life, but there are two things that he needs, a Bible because it is God that we seek, and a gun, because the world is dangerous in its new nature of world without Faith and Love.

The figure of Macphisto: meaning and symbolism

Present in the Zooropa tour together with Mr. The Fly it is the symbol of the new values that are taking the field and undermine the true values of the Faith. In particular Macphisto wants to indicate the temptation of the new era rather than being the symbol of consumerism (Mr. The Fly).

The phone is always an obsession for Bono, we will also see it in subsequent works, and in the 1993 tour will be Macphisto, the devil himself, to contact God, but there will be no answer. It's a sign that God is gone, leaving the field open to the new gods of the modern age, first of all to the devil and the sin. All the means that are well highlighted in ZooTV tour are the means which the devil uses to confuse and attract to himself humanity. And Macphisto takes the stage to reveal to all which is the true nature of what rules the world: it is only iniquity, because everything is the daughter of the devil.

But why the choice is right on Mephistopheles? Mephistopheles is a very powerful immortal demon, who has multiple powers all obtained by manipulating the forces of magic and can use these powers for everything. His powers range from transforming himself to using superhuman strength, from playing with human minds to altering the course of time.

Mephistopheles strengthens its power thanks to the evil in the kingdom of Man, on earth, but it is in his reign that he is more powerful, and if his physical form is destroyed he is able to regenerate not only himself, but also his own kingdom.

The main feature of Mephistopheles is to take possession of the soul, usually with a covenant, he having to have the "consent" to take possession of the soul.

In <u>Faust</u> Mephistopheles appears as a demon, a servant of Satan, but critics say he is not the kind of spirit that wants to corrupt the souls: in fact he only seeks the souls of those who are already damned. He himself is trapped in his own hell, and before tightening the pact he warns Faust, warns him of the consequences that will have to forget and betray the promise made to God. He is a spirit who wants the damned souls, but he is also a spirit that wants to save the fallen souls from mistakes and sins.

U2 will use again the phone to communicate with God: in <u>If God will send His angels</u> (<u>Pop</u>, 1997) we find the verse "God has got his phone off the hook, babe" where a girl tries to talk with God but the phone is disconnected.

The use the phone as a conduit to God emphasized by the character of Mcphisto, related with the Bible verse on the cover of <u>All that you can't leave behind</u> and tried with the phone call in "<u>If God will send His angels</u>" unequivocally leads to a single outcome: lack of communication.

Chapter 10

POP (Island, 1997)

After the silence after <u>Zooropa</u>, U2 finally released the album <u>Pop</u>. It is a strange album, which disappoints the expectations of fans: after the silence comes an album far too electronic. It should be noted that it is the third album in a row that follows the new sound, more modern, more commercial. Here the modernity of the music is taken to extremes and the album is almost forced to be so much different from what had been the U2 and the issues which anyway can be found in some songs, and bring U2 to their original message, although it is too often buried in excessive rhythms.

"Discotheque" still expresses the uncertainty of Man and the search for love.

Love is something impossible to control, maybe we can force it but we can not decide how to direct it because it is totally self-contained and we can find it everywhere, it goes everywhere.

In the fourth strophe the concept is openly stressed: "You get confused/ but you know it/ yeah, you hurt for it, you work for love/ you don't always show it". There is confusion in us, but in the end we know what Love is. The desire for love that is in us is infinite and often we ourselves are bearers of love, just do not want to show it not to feel different in a world where love is often relegated to second place.

"Let's go discotheque/ looking for the one/ but you know you're somewhere else instead/ you want to be the song/ the song that you hear in your head" means that we go looking for love in places that are not so obvious (the disco is not a church!) but in the end we know that it is not certain that we can find it there: our body is there but our mind is somewhere else and the thought is lost in a song that is in us, as an hymn of Joy and Love (once again we find here the split between body and mind, the first aimed toward the earthly and the material and the second aimed at the spiritual).

The next strophe deserves particular attention: "Love/ it's not a trick.../ you can't learn it/ it's the way you don't pay that's okay/ 'cause you can't earn it". Love is something important, so important that we can not even learn what it is.

It is already inherent in us; it is okay not to pay for Love because there is no way to earn it or earn enough to get it: only material goods and the false love can be bought. True love is priceless.

"Do you feel loved" is a song that can be read as a dialogue between Man and God. Man turns to God asking Him to take everything that belongs to him, everything that makes him a man, and he challenges Him to be able to keep him chained, bound to Him with no chance to break away.
God simply replies asking if he really feels loved in this way.
Still, the Man says to God to take everything, but this time it refers to everything that is not physical but mental, it is the imagination with its colours, it is the air with its odours, it is all that is Men's life.
"Take this tangle of a conversation/ and turn it into your own prayer" makes the idea of a God that leaves no choice but wants to establish Himself; Man challenges Him to recover what he really wants to say and replace these words with prayer, the only language that God knows and wants to impose.
"With my nailsunder your hide/ with my teeth at your back/ and my tongue to tell you the sweetest lie" point out that the Man eventually gives in to the insistence of this God, but it's all a joke: it is true that Man clings with all the strength God because it is He who asks him, but those are just lies that Man says. Behind an apparent submission Man still continues to live his life as he pleases.
Yet God simply asks if he really feels loved in this way.
At this point, between the angry and the resigned, the Man explains to God what love is for him: it is only a physical force that pushes a man and a woman standing together.

It is only when God continues to ask the Man if that's how he feels loved that comes out the true meaning of love, what Man really wants and expects, and thus sings the last strophe: "And it looks like the sun/ but it feels like the rain/ and there's heat in the sun/ to see us through the rain". Love becomes the sun while remaining as the rain; it is both heat and cold, salvation and temptation, Good and Evil. At last the sun is the warmth that allows us to survive the rain and that waits for us at the end of everything.
It cannot rain forever.

Let's see in _"Mofo"_ how the believer notices his loss, how he knows he wants to save him but keeps trying to do it the wrong way.
"Lookin' for to save my save my soul" is already in the first verse: I try to save my soul.
"Lookin' in the places where no flowers grow", I am searching in places where no flowers grow: they are in the dark area of the world where Good can not reign and with it Salvation too.
"Lookin' for to fill That God shaped hole" is in simple terms the need for a God. There had been bewilderment and detachment. God has left a void, a "God-shaped hole" that must be filled.
The concept of seeking salvation in the wrong place is taken up again in verse "Lookin' for baby Jesus under the trash". With the coming of Christ the way for Salvation has been opened, we are now seeking Jesus under the trash: the Man hopes to find salvation even where there is not any good. This verse, however, can have a second reading: why not interpret the search for Jesus in the garbage as an attempt to find the Good even where least

expected; the attempt to derive good from evil?

The third strophe is very significant:

Mother am I still your son, you know	It is almost a rhetorical question addressed to the Mother, who certainly will not deny any of his children.
I waited for so long to hear you/ say so	Long was the waiting to be recognized as children because long has been the search of one own being.
Mother you left and made me someone	At one time the sadness of abandonment, but also the certainty that thanks to abandonment there were possible the growth and maturity and the autonomy in the choices.
Now I'm still a child but no one tells me no	I'm still a child, as we all remain children in the eyes of a mother. However, it was at the stage of doubt and sin where every wish is granted.

In the last strophe we return to the search for truth. We ask to feel again emotions, asking the Mother that the soul could appeased because it does not look for wrong emotions in the wrong place anymore, we ask the Father to have rules to follow, because only the Father can control and give the right rules; we still asks the mother to show us finally the way because only the mother can bring us on the right path.

"If God will send his angels" is undoubtedly a song that opens itself, even in the middle of a so special album, to the classical theme of religiosity. It speaks of God's message and of how it is lived and passed: in the modern world are no longer faith, hope and love. Very few people carry with them these values but it is strange to see them as really referred to God and to other men. The song sings of the disappointment, the loss of hope and the abandonment: in this world is difficult even to turn to God in times of need and despair because He seems so far away and absent, we are almost ashamed to do so.

We are alone, no one commands us and decisions are only ours. Where is God, our reference? "Love took a train heading south": Love is gone.

Hence, the question that arises is: "if God would send his angels, or at least a sign, things would change and everything would be all right again?". The verse "It's the blind leading the blond" is a biblical quotation from Matthew 15:14: "Leave them; they are blind guides. If a blind man leads a blind man, Both will fall into a pit". If we go to those who, like us, are not able to open our eyes and see the Good there is no hope and we remain mired in sin.

Here returns also the reference to the phone call: "God has got His phone off the hook/ would he even pick it up if he could?". Once again God is unattainable, he unplugged the phone, but even if it were not so, however, we could not have the certainty of an answer. We are alone and we have to find the right way in the midst of all that is wrong around us.

The loss is well summed up in two lines of the third strophe, which are also a biblical reference: "So where is the hope, and where is the faith/ and the love?" are once again 1 Corinthians 13:13 (verbatim!). There is no longer anything because only with love we can have the joy around us (see thus the Christmas tree lights that light up, a symbol of the joy that comes back).

In the following strophe is expressed the difference between faith and religion: "Jesus never let me down/ you know Jesus used to show me the score" is Faith. Jesus does not leave anyone in pain and bewilderment and indicates what is right making us understand what is wrong.

"Then they put Jesus in show business/ now it's hard to get in the door" is religion, made of false preachers who praise God from television screens and who want to sell His image.

The more we follow this trend the more we get away from what God wants. And it is difficult to reach the goal.

We still wait for a wave of God and wait for His Angels.

"Staring at the sun" is a song about the presence of God and the search for God.

"Stuck together with God's glue": God is like a glue, is the bond that unites us all. We all have the same fate, we are ONE in God.

To stare at the Sun is to look at God and seek Him.

"I'm not the only one staring at the sun/ afraid of what you'd find":

we all look at the sun, we all tend to God even if what we could see scares us. "I'm staring at the sun/ not the only one happy to go blind": we all stare at the sun, and the sun blinds. We look at God and we do not mind at all being dazzled by His Light, remain blind and follow Him only with the Faith in Him.

The metaphor of the insect in the ear that we find in the second strophe symbolizes evil. The insect is the temptation that subtle, do not withdraw but continues to whisper in our ear. We can not dismiss it: the more we try the more it enters into us hurting us and dragging us into evil.

"Will we ever live in peace?": shall we be in peace, deliver us from temptation and sin? We stare at the sun to see Grace. In the two following strophes we reaffirm that God is always present. "Daddy just won't say goodbye": in doubt and uncertainty, in the struggle against sin, God does not want to leave.

"God is good but will He listen?": even in front of the immense goodness of God, we wonder if He'll be there to listen. But God is there and we still go back to stare at the sun, to become blind to find the Truth.

"Last night on earth" has in its title a reference to Revelation. The earthly life ends. There is uncertainty and, at the same time, the certainty that nothing can save us.

"She feels the ground is giving away" is the realization that something is changing. The ground gives way, the world as we know it is falling. But maybe it is better that way.

"The more you take, the less you feel" is once again the concept of the "the more you have the less you feel," more material things we possess the less we are spiritual; it is the triumph of materialism on the Spirit. Again, it is evil that triumphs over good.

"The less you know, the more you believe" emphasizes the triumph of ignorance meant as "no knowledge". To believe in something we must not know the meaning of it. We abandon ourselves to sin because in reality we do not know what it is and which are the consequences. It is okay so.

"The more you have, the more it takes today" is the realization that materialism is a vicious circle: it not only alienates us from God, but compels us to want more and more. We end up living like it's the last night on earth because we want everything at once. There is urgency because there may be no more time.

In the second strophe returns the theme of abandonment and rejection of God. We do not wait for the Saviour; we stand to wait, but do not really expect anyone even if the Sun rises and His Light illuminates us. God has not abandoned us, even if we do not want to believe it and we feel alone.

The third strophe is dedicated to the passage of time. The time almost gets out of hand until the hands stop and we realize that our time is up. Only now we come to understand that we missed something while the world continues to turn. Our mind goes crazy overwhelmed by doubt.

We are already projected into the future, as if to say that things will change.

"The future is so predictable/ the past is too uncomfortable" makes us understand how we live in a stalemate, the future being so predictable (nothing will change, we will continue to be alone and sinners) and the past is so uncomfortable (we lived in sin and

denied the right and we know it).
We should leave everything behind and live as if the world is ending, but this time not to have all but only to turn to the Saviour Who is there for us even though we did not expect Him.

"The playboy mansion" is, despite the title and the first feeling of impact, a song about religion and more specifically about the search for Heaven. The villa is initially a metaphor for the sinful material world and is where we can find everything and even more. Again it is stressed that in today's world we will lose the values that bring us closer to God and replace them with material values. With this materialism we try to build a new heaven but it is not enough.

"The banks feel like cathedrals/ I guess casinos took their place" are verses that bring the apex of the importance that is now given to material goods: there are no more cathedrals of the Spirit, but there are banks, the cathedrals of the new god that is money. Now casinos govern and casinos are the exact opposite of the cathedrals. Here returns to the dualism Spiritual/ Material.

The verse "Love come on down" is the space that is left to hope and to the desire of salvation. Yet the invocation is to Love to descend and help us.

"Chance is a kind of religion" again reiterates that religion has become something other. Everything is now based on luck, on having more rather than on being better.

There remains the invocation to Love as hope of salvation.

Note the next strophe: "don't know if I can hold on/ don't know if I'm that strong/ don't know if I can wait that long/ til the colors come flashing/ and the lights go on". Here it is summarized the yearning to Salvation and to God: we can not wait any longer, we are not strong enough to wait so long, to wait for the Light to turn on for us and overwhelm us with Its colours. We are not strong enough to wait for the Grace of God.

A period of sadness and shame will follow when we get aware of the mistakes made and of the bad choices, but it is the price to pay to return in the Grace.

The verses "And though I can't say why/ I know I've got to believe" explain why we always return in grace, they summarize the concept of faith: there is no reason to believe, we believe and that's it. And this is enough to save us.

At the end of the song we can see how the "playboy mansion" undergoes a radical transformation: it is no longer a place of vice and sin, but becomes a symbol of Heaven. The inner transformation that took place through the light that has filtered into the darkness of our lives allows us to see what is right and to go look for the Good. We find the verses "it's who you know that gets you through the gates of that mansion" that basically mean that only by knowing God He will open us the gates of Heaven, the Real One. It is therefore necessary to abandon materialism to go back to our origins, to be back to God.

Note how the verses "Then there will be no time of sorrow, then there will be no time for pain" can be found in Revelation 21:4: "And God shall wipe away all tears from their eyes; and there shall be no more death, neither sorrow, nor crying, neither shall there be any more pain: for the former things are passed away".

When crossed the gates of Heaven, in the knowledge of Good and

Grace, there will no longer be sadness and pain.

"If you wear that velvet dress" shows once again the contrast and the conflict between good and evil, here symbolized by the Sun and the Moon.

The moon reflects the light of the sun, then the image is ambiguous: on the one hand it is a reflection of Good, that Good which is also there when the sun has set; on the other hand it is the opposite of Good, it is what remains once the sun has set. If there is no more Good what remains is only the Evil.

Under the light of the moon the world seems to fade away, it seems us to be in the right even though we know that is not true; as children we go on asking for more because we know that nothing will be denied.

"Tonight the moon has drawn curtains" is the image of the moon that hides and disappears, and the reason why is explained immediately after: "sunlight fills my room". The sun is back in our lives.

Doubt and uncertainty remain, and the Man still wavers, arguing that, as clear and unmistakable in its being, the Sun is not like the moon, so charming and attractive. Evil attracts and flatters and it is too difficult to leave it.

Eventually once again the Good triumphs: "Tonight the moon is a mirrorball/ light flickers from across the hall/ who'll catch the star when it falls". The Moon is now a mirror and as such it reflects the light of a sun that has never disappeared but has remained in front of the moon just to be reflected. It is the Good that surrounds us.

The star that falls can have a double meaning: on the one hand the reference to Lucifer and to his fall. We can not get to him because no matter how strong and attractive Evil is, Good will always be stronger, so strong as to drag ourselves away. On the other hand, all the Angels are stars and it is impossible to touch the Angels, neither if they are the Angels of God running towards us to support us and guide us, because Faith is not to be tried or touched by hand, but it should only be Faith as Faith.

"Please" is, in the context of religious violence, a hymn to Love, understood as physical and spiritual; it is the demand that God makes to Man to stop praying for war and violence. God has nothing to do with all that. We are more and more violent, wars spread more and more (as concerns this point we can also consider the background of the war in Ireland) and Man fights convinced to act in the name of God, while God has only one desire: that Man should stop fighting and live in peace.

At the beginning we find the verses "you never knew love until/ you crossed the line of grace" that underline once again the importance of Grace. Only in Grace we can discover and understand the true Love.

The verses "you never felt wanted till you had someone slap your face" may be related to the custom that the Archbishop used to give a slap to the boys who, about twelve years old, became part of the true Catholics, after following the training in their infancy. It was almost a use of military determination, as if the Church was to be regarded more as a military association that must accept its militants with a ritual rather than the way to Heaven and something that allows us to live better.

Back again in this song the theme of the phone call. The phone is no longer the attempt to contact God because we feel alone and lost, but it is the culmination of Man. Only when it becomes necessary to seek God, the Man will lower himself to do so, because the Man is sure to be perfect and does not want to lower himself to ask for help.

"You never knew what was/ on the ground till they made you crawl/ and you never knew that/ the heaven you keep you stole" are the verses that refer to the human condition: the Man is sure to be perfect and invincible, but inevitably in the course of his life he meets someone who makes him understand the world in which he lives and which is the truth and realizes that where he lives is not Heaven, but only the Heaven he himself has created.

"Your sermon on the mouth" is a reference that is found in both Matthew 5:1-12 and Luke 6:20-26 (From the mountain Jesus makes a speech to the disciples, in which he indicates those happy the Heaven is intended for).

"Love is hard and love is tough/ but love is not what you're thinking of" are verses that support the double reading, the sensual one and the spiritual one. From the spiritual point of view it is the realization that Love is not what we have known on earth, but it is something bigger; it is strong and hard because it's difficult to catch and hold in oneself, but once we reach it its strength is such that we can no longer detach from it.

In the verse "Love is bigger than us" we find a confirmation of what was said before: Love is bigger than us and so is Love that controls us and guides us.

In the last two verses is expressed Man's frustration, a Man forced to give up his personal Heaven and forced to submit to something bigger. It is also the discomfort of a believer who has lost his way and his Faith: "Love is bigger than us/.../ you know I found it hard to receive/ 'cause you my love I could never believe".

It remains difficult to accept something we do not believe in, but simply the fact of calling Love by name leaves the door open to the Faith.

"Wake up dead man" is the anguished cry of those who wait for God to give meaning to their lives. In the context of the album, which sees materialism as a means to achieve happiness, the song can be read as a real "awakening" of a Man who realizes that he needs God and to Him asks to "wake up" to help him out of the darkness to find the meaning of life.

"Wake up dead man" may refer to Christ and to God, but also to Man himself: in this case it is God who asks the Man to awaken and find the right path. Faith has abandoned Man causing thus the current state of the world and only if Man awakes and returns to the Faith he can still hope for salvation.

Reading the lyrics it seems to me to read a dialogue between Jesus and the Man, with the Man who asks Jesus for help and the latter that makes him wake up.

Thus, in the first strophe the Man is conscious of his solitude, and calls for support to Jesus. He asks Him, almost as a child asks his mother, to be told a story and the story must be that of eternal life, the hope of salvation.

In the second strophe we find the reference to the Creation: "Your Father, He made the world in seven" is in Genesis 1:1-2:4 which is nothing but a description of the creation of the world by God.

We are so small and insignificant in comparison with the power above us that we can only stay motionless waiting. We can only ask Jesus to intercede for us with the Father, the Creator of the world and Judge of our lives.

The third strophe tells of the anguish of Man who is afraid not to be heard, to be covered by the confusion that surrounds him. Finally the relief and liberation come: "Jesus were you just around the corner?". We finally understand that we are never alone, that Jesus is always with us to listen to us and support us.

There is a program for us and we can not understand it and even if we ask that it is explained and re-explained to us the only answer we can get is "wake up dead man", awake dead man because it's time to open our eyes and understand. Awake dead man because now it is the time of God's Kingdom.

""Wake up, wake up dead man" is probably a reference to Ephesians 5:14 "... for it is light that makes everything visible. This is why it is said: "Wake up, o sleeper, rise from the dead, and Christ will shine on you"".

There are other references to the awakening in the Bible, and they are referred mostly to Christ Himself. See for example Psalm 44:23 "Awake, why sleepest thou, O Lord? Arise, cast [us] not off forever" or even, for "asleep" and "dead" in the Bible are often interchangeable, see Mark 4:38: "And he was in the hinder part of the ship, asleep on a pillow: and they awake him, and say unto him, Master, carest thou not that we perish?"

But why not see a reference to the Resurrection of Christ Himself? It is an invocation to Christ to wake up from the dead and bring us Salvation with His new life.

According to someone, the invocation is not only limited to Christ, but it is a foretaste of what will be the final cry after the coming of the new world: wake up you all to find yourself in God.

Chapter 11

ALL THAT YOU CAN'T LEAVE BEHIND
(Island, 2000)

Bono himself explained the reason for the title: "It is about the essential things, those that people say that are burned in the fire. In the scriptures they speak of fire through which to pass, of straw and wood that burn, and all that remains is precious stones. I love that idea. The eternal things are actually more sensitive, such as friendship and laughter. Love is not an easy thing, the only baggage you can bring is all that you can not leave behind".

After the musical experiments of the last album, now the band returns to its original sound, now we have "real" songs and not everything that can be built around. We return to the origins of U2. Only Elevation remains to stand out from everything and reminds us that we are not listening to a disc of the eighties, but we are in another time and in another era. They are still the new U2.

About the album, <u>Rolling Stone</u> magazine wrote: "Having spent twenty years pushing different styles, in <u>All That You Can't Leave Behind</u>, the band programs everything except what seems most important: the songs themselves. <u>All That You Can't Leave Behind</u> stands for an inner fire. Each track honours a melody so refined that each looks like an old permanent number. Because this is U2, the impact of these melodies is immediate, but every song has a resonance that does not disappear with repeated listening. <u>All That You Can not Leave Behind</u> is serious in its simplicity. The songs are not obscured by the excessive intervention of the production, but the band does not commit the common sin of boring foolishly people in the name of downsizing".

And, as always, this album is also the bearer of the themes and values of the identity of U2, including religion.

On a billboard on the background of the album cover we can read, among other things, "J33-3" as if it were a code for a departing flight when it is an obvious reference to a passage from the Bible (Jeremiah 33:3: "Let your cry come to me, and I will give you an answer, and let you see great things and secret things of which you had no knowledge"). The number is even jokingly considered the phone number of the Christian God, since "J" stands for the initial of "Jesus", ideally crucified at the age of 33 years and 3 months.

"Beautiful day" is a song that makes us stop to reflect on the beauty of the world and of life, not to forget who is the Creator; it is a song of hope and salvation.

In the first strophe we can see the loss: the heart is a germ, is able to flourish on any ground, as well as the love of God can take place in each of us. It is not, however, left the space to let it root and hence the static that becomes despair and abandonment.

"The heart is a bloom/ shoots up through the stony ground" is taken from Isaiah 52:3: "He grew up before him like a tender shoot, and like a root out of dry ground" and it also refers to the creation of Adam and Eve (from bare rock a bud from which comes life).

The verses "you thought you'd found a friend to take you out of this place/ someone you could lend a hand in return for grace" are full of disappointment: it was thought to have found someone who, through grace, could help us but it was only an illusion.

The day when the sky finally falls becomes so wonderful: again a metaphor for the end of the world. If the world ceases to exist then the sense of abandonment and suffering ceases too, and the day when this happens will be wonderful because we will be back in the Grace of God.

Very significant are the verses "Touch me, take me to another place/ teach me, I know I'm not an hopeless case": God is invoked to have Salvation. We call to have just a touch, we just need that He lights in us the light of faith so that it can lead us elsewhere, where no more confusion and doubt reign but only Grace.

We become aware that we are not hopeless cases, everything can be solved and there is room for everyone in the world to come.

We only need God to teach us the right way.

The following strophe becomes immediately a positive strophe: we no longer see the negative aspects and we are no longer in the stillness. Now everything is joy and movement.

We are witnessing a rebirth that is expressed in the image of the flood. Here there are two biblical references:

- "See the bird with leaf in her mouth" is Genesis 8:10-11: "[Noah] waited seven days more and again sent the dove out from the ark. In the evening the dove came back to him, and there in its bill was a plucked-off olive leaf! So Noah knew that the waters had lessened on the earth"

- "After the flood all the colours came out" is still Genesis 9:12-13: "God added: "This is the sign that I am giving for all ages to come, of the covenant between me and you and every living creature with you: I set my bow in the clouds to serve as a sign of the covenant between me and the earth"".

In the figure of the bird we can find a reference to Christ once again: according to legend, a bird mercifully pulled a thorn from the crown of Christ on the Calvary. In doing so, a drop of blood fell on its chest, colouring it red.

The invocation to the Father also puts an end to materialism: what we have is no longer necessary and we no longer need to know anything else, because all that we do not know we can feel in God and with God.

"Stuck in a moment you can't get out of is a song in which I read a dialogue between God and Man on the theme of Faith, doubt and salvation. The Man turns to God telling Him that he is not afraid of anything in the world and seeks only a "decent" song to sing, a hymn that is great enough to sing to God and to accompany him in his life.

"I am not afraid of anything in this world" can be found in Luke 12:4: "I tell you, my friends, do not be afraid of those who kill the body but after that can do no more".

God sees that Man falters and thus He reproves him and stirs him up "darling look at you/ you gotta stand up straight carry your own weight/ these tears are going nowhere". It is time for the Man to stop subjecting himselves (to doubt and sin), and he must stand up conscious of the weight that he should bring (his faults and sins). It is not with tears that we go along. It almost seems that God will spur Man to walk away from Him in order to walk alone. Immediately after He points out the moment of stagnation and uncertainty that the Man is experiencing: it is a moment from which we can not get out, it is needless to say it will get better, because this particular moment we are living does not allow us to go anywhere. God still seeks to spur the Man pointing out the doubt that chains him.

Man tries to explain to God that he still believes in Him and it is in the verses "I am still enchanted by the light you brought to me/ I still listen through your ears, and through your eyes I can see" that he underlines that: they well make the idea of a Man who feels one with God again. God's light enchants and attracts him and he still hears and sees everything through God. Man does not feel overwhelmed by sin and he still feels close to God. God's answer is always the same adding the fact that He points out to Man that it is not easy to stay strong in faith because going forward it will seem necessary to us even what we do not need now and that in any case will never be enough. Consumerism with its temptations is our way.

In the following strophe there is almost a justification for having yielded to sin: we have recklessly allowed sin to carry us. It all seemed nice and simple until we realized that behind this appearance many snares were hidden. To surrender has been a fall (still a reference to the fall of Lucifer, and thus a fall towards the Evil) that was just a fall to nowhere, because where there is no God there can be no life and no joy.

In repeating the usual answer, God adds some words that are a comfort to the Man because they infuse in him the assurance of salvation. The final strophe sings: "and if the night runs over/ and if the day won't last/ and if your way should falter/ along the stony pass/ it's a moment/ this time will pass" and summarizes how the Man will finally be able to exit the moment of stasis that is experiencing and will find faith in God; that faith that now is faltering. Although the night has the upper hand on light and even if we falter in the difficulties that surround us, in the end everything will pass, we will leave it behind to return to God.

"Elevation" is an hymn to God and to the raising of the Spirit. In the first strophe we still find the verses "high, higher than the sun/.../ I need you to elevate me here/.../.../ you elevate my soul" that are at one time to ask God to lift us up to His level and to know that He elevates our soul.

In the second strophe, which is repeated with only few variations as a chorus, is expressed the human condition: we have now lost control of ourselves and thus the way to salvation. We are now living underground, in the dark, and to make matters worse we continue to dig deeper and deeper. It remains, however, the presence of God who lifts us up and makes us feel as if we were flying high up in the sky, towards Him.

In the second strophe reappears the image of the star that suddenly appears, it is the presence of God that stands out. To Him we ask to move us towards the right, we tell him that we have a soul, even if now we are lost in our abyss (we are not able to sing because we can not spontaneously turn to Him) and that our ultimate goal is to elevate us.

At the end of the song as division between the last two refrains, we find the verses "Love, lift me out of these blues/ won't you tell me something true/ I believe in you" that are on the one hand the invocation to Love, on the other hand the yield in front of it.

We ask Love to let us out of our abyss and tell us what is true, but to Love we submit and we commit to It with the simple and unambiguous words "I believe in you".

"Walk on" is a song that, as the title suggests, aims to describe the journey of life. All in all it is a song that speaks of Heaven, that House that we do not know where it is but towards which we walk undeterred.

The song is about whatever it is we call God: to make sense of what we are and what we do we need to find a way through the obstacles that prevent us from advancing. We can not leave behind what we need, but it is within us that we must first seek and find what we need, which is only Love and God.

The song begins with the verse "Love is not the easy thing": Love is not so easy and obvious, it is something hard to find and hard to hold on tight. Speaking of Love intended as God it may be said, also taking the following verses, that the way to reach Him is impervious and we can not take anything except what we can not leave behind, which in this case is our being and the life we lived.

The second strophe exhorts us to be always strong, even in adversity, even when the darkness is so deep that it makes the light appear so distant as to seem unattainable. Again it means that often the evil and sin in which we are immersed are so strong to keep us away from the Light of God and make it appear so far that we have to give up to achieve it. It is in this moment that we must continue to move forward without looking back and thus reach the goal.

The lines of the following strophe must be underlined: "You're packing a suitcase for a place none of us has been/ a place that has to be believed to be seen". The verses express the concept of Faith: we must leave, take only one suitcase and go into the unknown. Only with Faith we can embark on the journey, because if there is no faith there is not even a safe destination.

"A place that has to be believed to be seen" is in John 11:40: "Did I not tell you that if you believed, you would see the Glory of God?".

The song goes on saying that, as we have forsaken the right direction to try to feel free, without any rule and submission, we must continue to walk because what we have, and what we are, can not be changed in any way. Only going on we can get to

Salvation.

I find important the verses "Home, hard to know what it is if you've never had one/ Home, I can't say where it is, but I know I'm going Home/ that's where the hurt is": our way leads us home, the instinct to move towards our house is innate in us. It can be difficult to know what "home" really is if we have never had one, it is difficult to understand the concept of Heaven if we have never believed in God. In any case, going on walking the final destination will be Heaven although it is impossible to say where it is: we can only feel inside the certainty that we are headed there, even if the path is not easy and can hurt us.

"Home - I can't say where it is, but I know I'm going" is in John 14:4-6: "Jesus said, "You know the way to the place where I am going". Thomas said to him, "Lord, we don't know where you are going, so how can we know the way?" Jesus Answered, "I am the way".".

The meaning of the song is clear from this reference: there's a place somewhere, we don't know where it is but we must go towards it, it is our destiny: one day we all will be in Heaven with God.

The song ends with a list of what we do not need, all that we can leave behind, which is pretty much all that is our life because we do not need anything at the end of our street.

In _"Kite"_ the uncertainty of life and the ignorance of Man are expressed. Like a kite in the wind we are pushed somewhere, but we do not know where.

"I'm not afraid to die/ I'm not afraid to live" is to understand how the Man leaves his own fate in the hands of someone else. To live or to die is the same because we do not know how our life will be and what our fate will be. It is the same also because there is a God both in life and in death.

The strophe "I want you to know/ that you don't need me anymore/ I want you to know/ you don't need anyone, anything at all" can be read in two directions: on the one hand it is the Man that turns to God, saying that He does not need either the veneration or the Man, that He is enough in Himself. On the other hand it can also be that God says to Man that he has no longer need of anything, not even a God. Anyway a sense of abandonment leaks out: Man and God are now separated, are no longer ONE, and the Man is abandoned to his fate as a kite in the wind.

The verses "don't wanna see you cry/ I know that this is not goodbye" at the end of a strophe that describes all the uncertainty of life, from the direction that will take up to its duration, leave a glimmer of hope for reconciliation with God. It is needless to cry, we well know that this is not a goodbye. Sooner or later the Man will find God again along his way and in any case he will find Him at the end of his life.

The verses "I'm a man, I'm not a child/ a man who sees/ the shadow behind your eyes" describe the loss of innocence, we see how children have a vision that is very different from that of adults. The children live on instinct and have God inside of them that makes it look all nice, right and simple. Adults live in the phase of doubt that leads them to choose between God and sin and they know that everything is not easy or obvious. Even God has

His mysterious and intelligible sides, and the shadow that lurks in Him can also be evil: if God is all He is both good and evil at the same time, He is also the tempter that puts us to the test in the hope of strengthening our faith.

The song ends with a question: "Did I waste it?", have I wasted my life (leaving it to drift)? We realize that we have not had enough and the reference is (with "rock stars" and "new media") to the consumerism that has departed us from the true values.

<u>In a little while</u> is a song that deals with the resurrection in Christ and the return to God while waiting for life in Heaven.

In the first strophe the verses "This hurt will hurt no more/ I'll be home, love" take back to the concept of Heaven as "home". It is the house where the love lives, the house in which no kind of evil can hurt us any longer.

In the second strophe the uncertainty returns: the night, with its sudden expansion, removes the living space of the day. Evil triumphs over Good. "I come crawling home" describes the desire to return to the Good. Repenting, coming from the state of sinners, we have to crawl back home, calling for forgiveness and longing for Heaven. At this point the question: "Will you be there?". Will there be God waiting for us and let us enter in His Grace or will we find the door locked, left to ourselves?

In the third strophe we have the transition from vice to virtue and here returns also a reference to the Holy Spirit.

The verse "In a little while, I won't be blown by every breeze" is a reference to Ephesians 4:14 ("Then, we will no longer be infants, tossed back and forth by the waves, and blown here and there by every wind of doctrine") and can be read in contrast to the previous song, Kite. As before we were drifted by the wind unaware of the direction that was taken, so now we no longer want to be transported at random but want to choose consciously our own way. So Friday brings us to Sunday: Friday is the beginning of the weekend, is the first evening dedicated to fun and transgression. From Friday, going on Saturday, we get to Sunday and we do it on our knees. On the Day of the Lord is on our knees that we enter His House, penitents, leaving behind the past days that we lived in sin. So the cycle is repeated endlessly reflecting the cycle of life itself: first innocence, then sin and doubt that follows and finally, with forgiveness, the return to the original state of innocence.

At this point, the Holy Spirit is mentioned, once again identified with a "she": "that girl she's mine" is a fact. The Holy Spirit has always been in us, we have always known it. Just a little time seems to be passed, but actually It is grown on us taking us along our way.

In the final part of the song the triumph of Love; Man dreams to fly, to live on a star (in the light of God). When the star falls dying in the night (the evil covers the Divine Light) Man follows the trail of light to remain attached to God. And this is Love.

In John 17 we find references to see Christ again "in a little while", such as in John 17:16 "In a little while you will see me no more, and then after a little while you will see me".

"Wild honey" is another song that speaks of God. The song uses the origins of humankind to explore what is the current awareness of God. Today we are docile and tame, and perhaps it is not what God had in mind for us: He is good but not docile and so we should be too. The part of us that is good but does not want to be tamed is the one in which there is the greatest awareness of God. The song also speaks of the Holy Spirit: as always, in everything we do, we feel Its presence and ask It to lead us with It in Its return to God.

The third strophe sings: "Did I know you even then?/ Before the clocks kept time/ before the world was made". The presence of the Holy Spirit is so strong that the question arises spontaneously: how long are we aware that It is there, do we know that It is with us since time and space hadn't existed yed, since we were originally in the infinite and eternal? As for the Spirit, this same consideration can be understood as a reference to God Himself: did we know Him even before the world?

In the following strophe we have the image of a sun that is no longer divine light that saves but becomes cruel, ready to burn us and then turn us away from Him. Again the Holy Spirit is ready to intervene: "from the cruel sun/ you were my shelter/ you were my shelter and my shade". The Spirit stands between us and the tempting sun as a shield and protects us from it and becomes our shadow to follow us and lead us in life. "You were my shelter and my shade" is in Isaiah 25:4: "You have been...a shelter from the storm and a shade from the heat".

"I'm still standing I'm still standing/ where you left me/ are you still growing wild/ with everything tame around you?" describe the complete submission to the Holy Spirit, that is bound to us but remains free in its being: we dare not move without It and we remain motionless in space and time. In the meantime the Spirit continues to change Its way of being: It is not tamed but continues to be wild, totally free in Its way of acting.

Finally, we still ask the Holy Spirit to guide us and lead us to the end with It, to bring us back to God.

"Peace on earth" is almost a cry of pain. We are tired of the world of pain that surrounds us, and we feel the need to have an Heaven on Earth too, the need that the Good and the Grace envelop everything and there will be finally peace.

Around us there is only destruction, but the attitude of Man does not change: we become monsters in order only not to be overwhelmed by other monsters. We forget about God and His rules to be the strongest in a wrong world.

In the fourth strophe Jesus is invoked because He would intervene and bring peace on earth allowing everyone to see and feel His Grace and to return to His Light.

Going forward with the text the invocation to Jesus is repeated. We still ask peace because the life of a person, as far as we known this person, is worth more than any ideal; we ask Jesus to save us, we are sinking in pain (victims and perpetrators at the same time) and we need His help to get back to the surface.

Jesus Himself taught us to sing for peace, but for how long this song is repeated we come to nothing. "The words are sticking in my throat" can mean on the one hand that the words can not come out of our mouths because the evil that surrounds us is so strong as to prevent us from invoking the Good; on the other hand we may think that words are locked in because even repeating the song the only thing we can do is go on repeating it endlessly because its words are ingrained in us.

The distress appears in verses "but hope and history won't rhyme/ I know what's it worth?/ this peace on earth": ours is a song of hope, but the hope is forced to remain so because the facts show that actually we can not have peace on Earth. We wonder if it is really worth to continue to sing, if we still have to ask for a peace that seems impossible.

Jesus can not remain deaf and there is only one thing to do: continue to hope and to invoke peace on earth.

"When I look at the world" expresses Man's attempt to see the world as God sees it. The Man speaks to God and asks Him what He really sees when He looks at the world.

"People find all kinds of things/ that bring them to their knees" refer to the false idols that Man creates to replace the true God in his material world.

Someone is still able to see the true God among all these idols and perhaps the verses of this song refers to Bono himself: he himself recognizes the true God, the One Who is able to change things just with His presence. So is he who tries to be like God and feel things as He feels and he does this trying to bring His message in every heart.

The verse "I can't see what you see/ when I look at the world" are almost a reference to I still have not found what I'm looking for: as then we were looking for something more so now we are looking for a higher level: we want to see the world as God sees it, but this is possible only rising at His same level.

In the third strophe the absence and indifference of God are expressed: the night is someone else's (sin dominates in the dark), confusion dominates and the Man gives in to sin, but God does not move, rather He turns away. In the context of the song we can better understand this attitude: it is not so much absence and neglect but rather a way of seeing and interpreting things; we humans think that God has abandoned us, but sometimes we do not think He sees things in a different way than us and therefore we do not necessarily have to think that He is not there. Rather, we have to think that this is part of a precise plan that He has for us.

Even more so, the urgent need to see the world as God sees it to avoid doubts and misunderstandings.

At the end of the song there is one more strophe that can be considered as referring to Bono himself: "I'm in the waiting room/ can't see for the smoke/ I think of you and your holy book/ while the rest of us choke". In the fog of bewilderment only one person, "I" that is Bono, is able to concentrate and not be like the others. His reference is the holy book, the Bible is the guide and the distinction.

The meaning of the final verses of the song, "tell me, tell me, what do you see?/ tell me, tell me, what's wrong with me" can again be extended to all human beings. We still ask God to lift us up to Him and tell us what He really sees when He looks at us and at the world, but above all He is asked what's wrong with us, we are so different from Him Who has created us as well.

"New York" expresses the theme of salvation. The city of New York became the symbol of what has become the world in which we live.

"In New York freedom looks like too many choices" is a key verse, emphasized at the very beginning of the song. The life faces us up with choices and the more we have choices the more we feel free. Too many, however, are the voices that surround us, that confuse us and not allow us to make the right choice. Then we end up with trying different roads. It is then described everything that we can find and get in New York, which becomes by extension all that the world offers.

Once again we are surrounded by materialism and linked to it.

Right at the end of the song the lifeline in the verse "In the stillness of the evening/ when the sun has had its day/ I heard your voice a-whispering/ come away child": the night is quiet and the sun is about to set. In this transition phase that symbolizes the passage Good/ Evil, and that stands to mark the fine line the Man walks on, a voice breaks and with a simple whisper brings us back in the right.

"Come away child": the Father turns to His son to take him away from vice and sin and bring him back with Him in the right.

"Grace" is a beautiful description of the Grace known through Faith. It is therefore also a song dedicated to the Holy Spirit that is the bearer of grace.

The Holy Spirit is the means by which we come to God, then is He, together with Grace, Who takes all our sins, covers all our shame and removes the stain from our souls.

The first lines of the second strophe clear very well what the song refers to: "Grace, it's the name for a girl/ it's also a thought that changed the world". Grace is a name (let's remember here that the Holy Spirit is often identified with a "she"), but above all Grace is a simple idea that has the power to change the world. The Holy Spirit is in us, but It is also a universal thought and through It our world changes and we move from the material to the spiritual, we pass from sin to God.

There is a verse in the song that is repeated three times with a little variation and is an exact description of the Holy Spirit and of the Grace of God. We find, first of all, "Grace finds goodness in everything" which then becomes "Grace finds beauty in everything" and finally "Grace makes beauty out of ugly things".

At first, Grace is a passive presence that simply finds the positive in the negative: in everything there is something good and beautiful and it is Its job to find it. In the last variant proposed Grace becomes an active presence that no longer limits Itself to find what is good but creates it directly. With Its strength Grace is able to transform into something beautiful even what is not; It even manages to turn evil into good.

Two verses of the fourth strophe are also of particular note: "Grace, she carries a world on her lips/.../ she carries a pearl in perfect conditions". The Grace of God imposes Itself to the world, controls it, and with a single word can change everything. At the same time Grace, through the Holy Spirit, is the bearer of the Word and of the Kingdom of God that can only be perfect and precious, a rare and pure pearl.

In the song there is then a perfect description of God and of the

Love He has for us:

- "Grace, she takes the blame" is the Messiah on the cross. Christ died because He took on Him the blame for our sins.
- "It's also a thought that changed the world" is the incarnation of God: from pure thought to material, from infinite to finite being.
- "She travels outside of karma": considering the "karma" as the evil, in karma we deserve everything, including evil, while in the Grace we have only positive things and nothing bad. But even considering the Karma as what it is more properly, that is we have only what we deserve, Grace is something that goes beyond this and is to have more than we deserve.
- "Grace, she carries a world on her hips" refers to the fact that Grace protects us as Its children because It sees us as such. Even Jesus refers to us as the children of God.
- "What left a mark no longer stains" is a clear reference to the stain of sin.

Through Grace we get more both from God and from the others. When we respond to negative actions with positive actions, we transform the action into a perfect pearl and this transformation can change the world. This is the only true message of love that we have to consider, which is also the only one true commandment: love your neighbour.

Let's underline the biblical references:

"She carries a pearl in perfect conditions" is Matthew 13:45-46: "The kingdom of heaven is like a merchant looking for fine pearls.

When he found one of great value, he went away and sold everything he had and bought it".

"What left a mark no longer stains" is not exactly a biblical quote, but rather an allusion to Isaiah 1:18, "Though your sins are like scarlet, they shall be as white as snow".

"The ground beneathe her feet" is another song about Man's loss and his finding again with the help of God.

The Man realizes that he has followed and worshipped something or someone he believed was giving him happiness.

"She made me real" is on the one hand to feel alive thanks to the sensations that we feel, on the other hand is to become real and break away from the spiritual to fall into the material reality.

After this first awareness we realize the loss and confusion that appropriate us: "now I can't be sure of anything/ black is white, and cold is heat/ for what I worshipped stole my love away". The false idols that we worshipped turned us away from the true values and from the right, so now evil seems good to us, but we are realizing this. Above all, we realize that the false idols have taken the Love away from us moving us away from It.

The last two strophes are words that God tells to Man to make him go on the road even if in doubt because he still will not be alone.

"I won't rest until you're found" is the key phrase: I will not stop looking for you until I find you. God is sure to be able to save His children and will continue to accompany them until they have found the right path. Similarly, the Man is sure that he will search God until he will find Him the way down his street.

"Let me love you true, let me rescue you/ let me lead you to where two roads meet/ o come back above/ where there's only love". In these verses is the key: God lowers Himself to ask Man the permission to love him and save him, the permission to take him to that place where good and evil meet to bring him back towards Good, on the surface. On the surface there will be only Love because there Man will be back with God.

Chapter 12

HOW TO DISMANTLE AN ATOMIC BOMB
(Island, 2004)

The new album does not say anything new compared to what U2 have said so far. The accents are now, however, more mature, full of what they have learned and gained so far; the band gathers around it different expectations after the partial return (with <u>All That You Can't Leave Behind</u>) to the sounds of the '80s.

It is not a purely conceptual album, but for its most it deals with a world that is at the crossroads of its existence. The central themes are love and war, peace and harmony, death that is always lurking nearby, returning thus to the mix of the usual topics, such as politics, love, religion.

The band returns to its roots with the return of the great hymns that characterized their work through the 80s.

We are facing a cinematic album that is also able to put fans and critics agree, happy to raise again the band to the Olympus of music. But in fact, the album has a decidedly conservative aspect after the risks taken for most of the last decade, now U2 hold down their sense of adventure by consciously removing the great sense of humour that has characterized their production since Achtung Baby and returning to the great sound and the sincere feeling of their work of the 80s.

We see thus a "rebirth" after being lost in modernism and in the dazzling disco music; the group is again the social conscience of the music, as it was in its origins. In an attempt to revive the old themes and concepts and to pass them as in their classic work, they almost exaggerate, perhaps removing too much of the audacity of the rhythm and of the strength of the songs. They succeed in their aim, however, sending us deep emotions and their message.

"Vertigo" is considered by Bono himself the first single from their first album. It resumes undoubtedly their first Out of control and Stories for boys.

It is the opening song on the disc, and with the first verses we see how it is related to the closure of the album, in a perfect circle, "unos, dos, tres, catorce!" is a biblical reference. It is stated as 1 = first testament; 2 = second book; 3 = third chapter; 14 = verse fourteen, that is "And God said unto Moses, I AM THAT I AM: and he said, Thus shalt thou say unto the children of Israel, I AM hath sent me unto you". I AM is none other than God, more precisely the name given to God by God Himself. And after this beginning the album ends with a song called <u>Yahweh</u>, which is still the name of God, and the circle is closed.

Looking more closely at the song, we can still see how God is invoked to help us resist temptation: everything is dark, all is temptation ("The girl with crimson nails/ has Jesus round her neck" emphasizes that even a highly spiritual sign as the crucifix can become a symbol of temptation, the lure of the flesh), only with the intervention of God, Who gives us something that we really feel, we can resist.

In the first strophe is expressed the confusion that pervades the Man: the darkness takes the place of light; in the head a confusion that does not even allow to control the heart.

"A feeling is so much stronger than/ a thought" are verses that leave a glimmer open: the mind is thought and thought is lost in doubt but there is something stronger that can overcome the thought and this is what we feel inside. We can abandon the same the right path to fall into doubt even if our soul will always remain intact: "And though your soul/ it can't be bought/ your mind can wonder".

The chorus repeats that we live in a place called "vertigo": the name itself gives a sense of loss and insecurity. Still there is a presence, God, that even in this place is able to give us something that can touch our soul.

The last time the chorus is repeated it presents some changes: "I'm" becomes "we're". No longer something that can be referred to a single person, but something that can be extended to everyone. And in fact every Man lives in vertigo.

"It's everything I wish I didn't know" becomes "lights go down and all I know" and express no more the loss to find in a place all that we would not find, but the consciousness of being in the dark and know one thing for sure.

"Except you give me something I can feel" becomes "Is that you give something", that linked to the verse above expresses the strength of the belief that God is the only One that can really give us something and make us feel something.

In the second strophe again the theme of the triumph of good over evil in the metaphor of the light that pierces the night. This time the night is described as something physical and concrete, which can be torn off, and the stars that illuminate it become the blinding flashes of a bullet fired into the sky to make it rain light.

The last part of this strophe, linked to the following strophe brings us back a bit to the themes of <u>Zooropa</u> and <u>Pop</u>, linking the materialism to the spiritual. The stars shine while they hear playing. Pop stars become idols, the false idols that take the place of God. "I'm asking for the cheque" is a fine example of how the new money God trumps everything and the only thing that really matters is to have money, be with the new God.

The glimmer of hope is given by the image "Jesus round her neck": in a false world we still bear the symbols of faith because God is not dead, God is always with us.

"All of this can be yours/ just give me what I want/ and no one gets hurt" refers to the temptation of Christ in the desert by Satan, specifically the words of Satan in Luke 4:7: "So if you worship me, it will all be yours".

The concluding lines are the surrender of Man before God, a Man who consciously wants to find the right way: "I can feel your love teaching me how/ your love is teaching me how, how to kneel". The Man can finally feel something inside that fills the soul and takes him away from consumerism: it is God Who is teaching him to kneel before Him because it is there that the we penitent and filled with hope kneel and not in front of the false idols that surround us.

"Vertigo", the dizziness, is also that feeling we get when, in the Church, we become one with God. We should remember that Bono is a Christian and is attentive to the rites of the Church, to what they mean and what they broadcast. But why not intend the dizziness as that we feel on the brink of an abyss? We are all on the brink of the Fall; if we give in to temptation and don't turn to God, the Fall is our destiny. With God we can hope again, because He allows us to feel and really teaches us how to kneel down to get to the truth.

In *"Miracle drug"* Faith and science merge, something very difficult to do, always. Bono points out that even through science God is present to perform His miracles and with His Perfect Love anything is possible.

The song is a dialogue with God and a prayer to God.

In the first strophe is expressed the desire to be like God and in God and again we would like to see everything through His eyes and we would like to know all those things that He alone knows, the mysteries of His message and our destiny.

"I want to hear you when you call" is on the one hand the desire to be able to detach ourselves from the world in which we live every time God asks; the desire to be able to choose the spiritual side of life abandoning the material one; on the other hand the verse can be read as a reference to the call: we want to be ready when God calls us to Himself, we want to be already free from sin and prepared to receive Him only.

Only through God we can find our way, in Him are the songs to sing and the miracles, which are a real drug or, better, a wonderful drug that cures our lives and our souls.

The following strophe points out how the world around us has no limits, science and heart, material and spiritual, have no bounds but also in this perfection is something that does not work and it is the absence of God.

We have to quote the next strophe:

"I am you and you are mine"	As in the song <u>One</u> returns here the theme of the union with God: Man and God are like one same thing.
"Love makes nonsense of space/ and time, will disappear"	With Love time and space disappear because Love is infinite and eternal.
"Love and logic keep us clear"	Love and logic help us to stay away from sin.
"Reason is on our side, love"	With Love also the reason is back in the right being back in tune with the heart and with God

In verses "beneath the noise/ below the din/ I hear a voice/ it's whispering/ in science and in medicine" we see how the echo of God's presence can also be felt in the noise and how this voice whispers its presence in science and medicine as in the Faith.

"I was a stranger/ you took me in" is Matthew 25:34-35: "Then the king will say to those on his right, 'Come, you who are blessed by my Father; take your inheritance, the kingdom prepared for you since the creation of the world. For I was hungry and you gave me something to eat, I was thirsty and you gave me something to drink, I was a stranger and you invited me in..." (note the King James Version, which says "and ye took me in").

Again we find the transition from a lower level of love to a higher one: as mentioned earlier, the Greeks recognized four types of love (Phileo - brotherly love, Storge - parental love, Eros - romantic or sexual love, Agape - love as love in itself); Bono says here that he is trading romantic love for a higher love which he defines a "miracle drug": the highest Love is that of God and that comes to us through science and medicine as a drug that works wonders. The verses are: "I've had enough for romantic love/ I'd give it up, yeah, I'd give it up/ for a miracle, a miracle drug".

In the verse "God I need your help tonight" there is the essence of the song and of life. It is a desperate turn to God knowing that it is the only One able to save us. "I need your help," is the surrender of Man who recognizes himself weak and inferior in front of the Love of God, Who is the Saviour. In the din, in the confusion that surrounds us, there is always a voice that stands out and whispers to us. We find it in all things, in nature as in science as in everything else, it is the voice that guides us and makes us part of the miracle of life.

"Sometimes you can't make it on your own" are all words that God Himself addresses to Man. As if in answer to the previous Miracle drug here is God that speaks to Man and makes him realize that he is not alone and should not rely only on himself.

In the first strophe God reproves the Man because he wants to pretend to be strong enough, while in the second strophe He offers to be with him and share the difficulties. More explicitly, in the second strophe, with "Listen to me now/ I need to let you know/ you don't have to go it alone" God invites Man to listen to His words and convince himself that it is not alone on his path.

In the chorus returns once again the image of the phone call to God; God is absent or, better, He is there but does not want to answer.

"And it's you when I look in the mirror"	Man is the reflection of God because it is in His image and likeness.
"And it's you when I don't pick up the phone"	God does not answer the phone when the Man tries to get in touch with Him: God is absent, but perhaps He wants to leave the Man free in his choices.
"Sometimes you can't make it on your own"	There are times when the Man can not do it by himself, he is not enough in himself and needs God.

The next strophe describes the eternal conflict between Man and God: they are One, the same thing, but they always try to impose one on the Other. God is greater but the Man tries to be even better and this deep contrast is well expressed in the verses "If we were not so alike/ you'd like me a whole lot more": the Man and God are so similar that if they were a bit more different Man could love God without continuing to fight and oppose Him.

"I know that we don't talk" reiterates the lack of communication between Man and God, but the following verses underscore also how this state of non-communication has become boring and now the use of the songs is stirred: songs are the best way, the most direct and intimate way, to express ideas and feelings.

Significant are also the verses "Where are we now?/ I've got to let you know/ A house still doesn't make a home/ don't leave me here alone": there is uncertainty in the relationship between Man and God, and The Latter feels the need to remind the first that a house is not a real home, meaning that walls are not enough to create an ideal environment, but it is important to have all the rest and not be alone. God asks Man not to abandon Him so that he can build with Him that home that is peace, shelter and protection. Nothing of this can be done by ourself, we can at most pretend to do it, but it is only with God on our side that we will succeed in everything.

"Love and peace or else" is a song that relates once again to the relationship between Man and God. It certainly speaks of love and peace, but we must more deeply interpret it as living in peace after having found God and shared His Love.

The song also speaks of forgiveness and how the world is destined to go more and more worse if we do not turn to love and we do not desire and seek peace in ourselves. The search for peace and love is not easy; it means first of all give up a lot to live according to the teachings of Christ and means forgiveness to live a life in peace with oneself and with others.

The Man asks God to "lay down" His Love, to bring It down to earth to defeat sin ("we're gonna break the monster's back") and God says to Man that from the very moment in which He gives him life He hopes to see him already old and above all with a "brand new heart", a heart that through all the experiences of life has become "brand", precious and perfect.

Facing this the Man feels weak, he does not know if he can manage to do it because it is not easy nor simple to kneel. He can only give his heart to God in order to let Him accept it or break it.

We just need love and peace and this is expressed in the strophe "Lay down/ Lay down your guns/ All your daughters of Zion/ All your Abraham sons" that, inspired by the story of Abraham, well gets the idea of the trust we must put in God: as Abraham was about to kill his son to offer him to God but the Latter stopped his hand, so we must be ready to sacrifice everything for the Love of God, conscious of the fact that He can intervene at any time to stop us. This takes away a great part of the sense of sacrifice, however, while not necessarily God will intervene to stop us. The conscious choice to give up the things we love for the Love of God will always have an high value.

While the Man invokes love and peace, God reassures him once again by saying not to fight and emphasizes His presence in the lines "we can talk this thing through/ it's not a big problem/ it's just me and you": God does not leave Man alone, but He wants to deal with problems together with him ("we" and not "you" or "I") talking about them to make them less great.

Here returns once again the theme of the phone call, but this time it is God Who propose it, and not only this time He will be on the other end of the line, but He Himself will be calling.

The song ends with the eternal question that haunts Man: "Where Is the Love?" Man aims to peace and love and peace and love are what Man needs.

"Lay down your treasure" is Matthew 6:19-21: "Do not store up for yourselves treasures on earth, where moth and rust consume and where thieves break in and steal; but store up for yourselves treasures in heaven, where neither moth nor rust consume and where thieves do not break in and steal. For where your treasure is, there your heart will be also".

"City of blinding lights" is a search for God among sins and temptations with the consciousness to have lost Him and the hope of finding Him again.

Analysing the song on the detail we can see:
- "The more you see the less you know/ the less you find out as you go/ I knew much more then than I do now."

A strophe in which it is realized that going forward in life we learn a lot and make a lot of experiences, but we do not necessarily know or know more as we go forward over the years... the more we grow, the less we know, given that the experience of life takes us away from the state of original innocence. In practice, while growing we get away from God and we do not get the answers we seek just because we are more and more distant from God

- "A city lit by fireflies/ they're advertising in the skies/ for people like us".

The sky is lit by fireflies, they are stars that light the way, they are perhaps the angels of divine light that shine and show us the way; the sky is what we must aim at because it is our last destination and the light shows us the way through the sin to new life.

- "And I miss you when you're not around/ I'm getting ready to leave the ground".

From these verses shines through all the sadness. We can feel the lack of the presence of God and we are ready to leave this earthly life to be with Him. By reading these verses relating more closely to Bono's personal life, we could tie their meaning to Bono's mother, who since her death followed and influenced Bono's lyrics: it is of his mother and not only of God that he feels the lack, and it is to be back in Heaven with her that he is ready to leave our world.

The city lights are blinding and there God is magnificent: the light has triumphed again over darkness. Similarly we can interpret the "City of blinding lights" as Heaven Itself. Heaven is all shining with light, there is no room for darkness and God is wonderful in His Kingdom. Man, ready to leave his world, has reached God in His Kingdom.

- "I've seen you walk unafraid/ I've seen you in the clothes you made/ can you see the beauty inside of me?/ what happened to the beauty I had inside of me?".

Here too we find a reference to Bono's mother, she is dead, the son has seen her leave... with the death of his mother faith falters, he realizes he has lost it... he asks thus what happened to his faith, to the beauty that he had inside.

More in general, it is still a reference to the passage from innocence to adulthood: in the time of innocence in Man there was only beauty and now the Man asks where is the beauty, injured by experience and sin, and in particular he asks God if He can still see the beauty inside of him.

- "Time time/ won't leave me as I am/ but time won't take the boy out of this man"

With this strophe the present is bound to the past. It can still be interpreted in a more personal way, referring to the fact that despite the time passes, he still feels the absence of his mother, and will always remain a child for her.

There may be, however, a more general and religious interpretation: "I" represents everyone, we realize that time changes people, that we grow and make experience of the world: there is the loss of innocence, of the original condition present in children. From an adult can never be brought out the child: the innocence is gone, forever.

- "The more you know the less you feel/ some pray for others steal/ blessings are not just for the ones who kneel/ luckily"

Here it is again stressed that God's Grace is for everyone. The Bible itself says that the righteous are not perfect, but Grace is for them. And Grace is also suitable for those who are not on the right either because they do not follow the teachings of Christ or because they have forsaken the right way that is in God.

"Blessings are not just for the ones who kneel/ luckily" is found in

Matthew 5:44-45: "But I tell you: "Love your enemies and pray for those who persecute you, that you may be sons of your Father in heaven. He causes his sun to rise on the evil and the good, and sends rain on the righteous and the unrighteous".

"All because of you" speaks of rebirth, of how the Man realizes that it is only thanks to God that he exists and he is what he is. In the first verse ("I was born a child of grace") is stressed how we are born in the Grace of God and then we try to leave the state of grace to see what lies beyond. The Man knows to be born in the Grace but do not know nothing of the place from which he comes. The only clear thing is the beautiful face of God. There is no illusion and everything looks uglier because we are forced to go away from that place to live our life.

In the second strophe the presence of God is clear: God becomes the moonlight; it is no longer the sun that drives us but it is the moon that watches over us in the dark, but its light is cold and distant. The strophe is: "I saw you in the curve of the moon/ in the shadows cast across my room/ you heard in my tune/ when I just heard confusion". God is everywhere, in the cold light of the moon, even in the shadows that the cold moonlight casts... God is also in Evil, He can hear our frequency even if there is only confusion around us, and bring us back.

"I like the sound of my own voice" suggests the belief that we can make it on our own: now we have left God behind and the only thing we hear is our own voice that now is our guide. We believe that by acting on our own we can not make mistakes and we are convinced to be enough to ourselves.

The lines "I'm not broke but you can see the cracks/ you can make me perfect again" are almost autobiographical: in contrast to all the lost people, Bono won't let himself be overcome, he can see the lacerations caused by doubt and wrong choices but God will make him perfect again. The autobiographical note, however, can be extended to everyone in the sense that everyone has lived his own experiences in a different way and in a different way has been marked, but with God we can find the perfection of our original state.

"All because of you/ I am": in the same album can be found a song (<u>Yahweh</u>) who has as title the Hebrew name of God and the song <u>All Because Of You</u> which translates His name with a good English rendering. See on Exodus 3:13-14: ""But", said Moses to God, "when I go to the Israelites and say to them, "The God of your fathers has sent me to you" , if they ask me, "What is his Name?" what am I to tell them?" God replied, "I am who I am". Then he added, "This is what you shall tell the Israelites: I AM sent me to you."". This particular links this song to the first song on the album, <u>Vertigo</u>, the opening of which refers to "1": the Old Testament; "2": the second book (Exodus); "3": the third chapter; "14": verse 14, "I am who I am". It can not be a mere coincidence. The verses "An intellectual tortoise/ racing with your bullet train" tell about the eternal challenge between God and Man, with the realization that not only we can not be greater than God, but we can not even get close to being as Him: we are intellectually as turtles, while God is a train that goes like a bullet... our mind is finished, it has its limitations, it moves slowly while God is infinite, He has no limits, He can do everything at once.

There is a sense of cyclicity in the song that can be linked also to the memory of his mother. Thus we have the cycle of birth and death, "I was born in grace" at the beginning and "And I want back inside" at the end. It is the rebirth in God and the return to Him, as well as the physical birth from the mother to the final return to her.

"Everything was ugly but your beautiful face" further emphasizes this duality: the world is difficult and hard, only the mother's face is beautiful in the midst of everything else, she is a reference that gives support and strength. But it can also be the face of God, Who even under the greatest difficulties and the greatest mistakes is present and gives us hope and support.

The last strophe deserves to be mentioned as the most significant of the song and it is also the strophe that let the circle close. "I'm alive/ I'm being born/ I just arrived, I'm at the door/ of the place I started out from/ and I want back inside": we have survived in the world and now we have come to a true rebirth, we have arrived at the gates of the place from which we came and that's where we want to go back.

At the end of life we reborn in Christ and return to the origin, in that Heaven from which we come, in the Grace.

"A man and a woman" deals with the contrast between earthly love and spiritual love.

The sensual love attracts because it is sweet and involving, but true love is the only one that we can not lose and we can not lend because only true Love maintains unchanged the beauty fixing it in its innocence.

We are not free to choose between the two different kinds of love ("Love" versus "Romance") being attracted by both. The distance that creates between a man and a woman is mysterious, as mysterious is the power of Love. It is here that sensual love and spiritual love meet.

"You can run from love/ and if it's really love it will find you" describe the force of love: even if we try to get away from it if it is true love we will not be able to get rid of it. Only God's Love is true love, and even though we try to move away to live in the world and in earthly love it will continue to follow us to get back to us.

The fusion of sensual love and spiritual love can also be seen in the strophe "Brown eyed girl across the street/ on Rue Saint Divine/ I thought this is the one for me/ but she was already mine": the girl is described in earthly terms (describing the eyes, where she is and the thoughts that she causes) but then we realize that she is not an unknown girl. Here returns the reference to the Holy Spirit as a female figure: when we meet the Holy Spirit on our journey we meet with a love so great that we can not realize that it was already part of our being.

We have also to note the verses "I've been trying to feel complete again/ but you are gone and so is God/ the soul needs beauty for a soul mate/ when the soul wants, the soul waits": in giving ourselves away to the sensual love an attempt was made to feel complete as we felt before discovering that we are not enough to ourselves. But it is not enough and we understand that both God and the Holy Spirit are gone: the soul needs a beauty that may be given only by another soul that completes it. This can only be God, and our soul is happy to wait because only then it will feel complete in the Love of God.

"Crumbs from your table" deals with the Church and is also a dialogue between God and Man. God speaks to Man and notes how often from the brightest star comes the biggest black hole (scientifically, in the process of stellar death a star passes through a phase of supernova, brilliant star, through the white dwarf phase, cold and dying, to the final formation of a black hole). From the point of view of a religious reading we note that Lucifer was the brightest angel then he fell giving rise to hell, in total darkness.

God asks why the Man has sold his soul wanting to be rid of Him when He has always been there. The Man asks God not to be abandoned, but then why is the Man to abandon God?

The refrain, "You speak of signs and wonder/ I need something other/ I would believe if I was able/ but I'm waiting on the crumbs from your table" repeats Man's answer and there is a direct attack on the Church and to its way of thinking and acting: we no longer believe in a Church that only promises miracles and signs but there is nothing more: the believer wants more, he wants a practical demonstration of what is preached. If the Church is not the first to act and "perform miracles", the believer turns away. Although we can not believe, the separation is not complete however, and we expect to be able to have at least something, the crumbs of the great promises.

"I would believe if I was able/ I'm waiting on the crumbs from your table" is Matthew 15:21-27: "Leaving that place, Jesus withdrew to the region of Tyre and Sidon. A Canaanite woman from that vicinity came to him, crying out, "Lord, Son of David, have mercy on me! My daughter is suffering terribly from demon-possession". Jesus did not answer a word. His disciples came to him and urged him, "Send her away, for she keeps crying out after us". He answered, "I was sent only to the lost sheep of Israel". The woman came and knelt before him. "Lord, help me!" she said. He replied, "It is not right to take the children's bread and toss it to their dogs". "Yes, Lord", she said, "but even the dogs eat the crumbs that fall from their masters' table".

But it is also a reference to Luke 16: 19-21: "Now there was a certain man of great wealth, who was dressed in fair clothing of purple and delicate linen, and was shining and glad every day. And a certain poor man, named Lazarus, was stretched out at his door, full of wounds, desiring the broken bits of food which came from the table of the man of wealth; and even the dogs came and put their tongues on his wounds". Considering also the following verses of Luke, we can read the whole thing as a warning: only the deserving will be with God. Those who are rich and do not make the right use of money will not be with God, with their money will not even buy the Kingdom of Heaven: yet a criticism to the Church that with its richness merely preaches the right but does not act accordingly.

In the song God goes on remembering to Man how he was perfect in his state of Grace, and how then he has exchanged Love with Hate learning to hurt without any problem.

Finally, God remembers to Man that is not his the power to decide of his life: "Where you live should not decide/ whether you live or whether you die". In the end it is God who comes back and leads the Man, deciding in his place because He has the reins of life. Again, the Man asks for something more than words to believe and in the end he stands waiting in hope of an answer.

"One step closer" is a song about the loss of Man and about his realization of being a sinner up to his will to seek God.

The beginning of the song talks about the loss: what is real and right is not far from us, we are still on the road of hope, we are not yet lost in sin. The image of the bridge and the tide that takes away everything refers to the evil's strength to drag us down and it is from that bridge that separates good and evil that we want to throw down, towards the evil, where there is everything that we think our.

So the first chorus "One step closer to knowing" can be interpreted as being closer to the knowledge of the world, of the evil and sin rather than being related to the knowledge of God.

Even the second strophe expresses the confusion: we are at a busy intersection and we can neither go forward nor back. We are obliged to choose, but the confusion is so great that we do not know what to do. We are able to perceive the future as a distant vision and there remain only the echoes of a few lights that are going out: we are letting ourselves go to sin losing the right path. And the knowledge of evil is getting closer.

In the last strophe there is the recovery and the coming out from sin: "I'm hanging out to dry/ with my old clothes" symbolize the resurface from the raging torrent that swept up and dragged us into sin. The clothes are always the same because it is still us, we have not changed but we are just more mature.

The image of the sting of the rose refers to the image of Jesus's crown of thorns. We too are stung and bleed; this brings us closer to Christ and we understand that only a heart that loves can really hurt us, and that is the Heart of God.

Here the last chorus refers to true knowledge: we are not closer to knowing the evil, but we are getting closer to knowing God.

"Original of the species" is once more a song centred on religion. It is a dialogue between God and Man: knowing what the destiny of Man is, God almost requires him to remain somehow a child, innocent, at least in some corner of his being. Life, and death above all, are not as beautiful as birth and childhood. The Man knows that God gives him everything, but there's always something missing, something that will make seem too little everything he has. At the end we realize that the only thing we really miss is God and of Him we always want more.

The song, however, is also a song of Christ: He is the first and the original, He has come to save us and for the resurrection. He is the first in a long line that will follow Him and will be like Him.

We kneel before Christ and of Him we want everything.

Wherever He goes He shouts to the world His message without feeling embarrassed and without fearing the consequences. To Him, the One and the Original, we mortal beings give everything except the one thing He really wants: our soul to be His, and not belong to evil and sin. As sinners we can not free ourselves from the yoke of evil, and for this reason we kneel before Him, and of Him we want more and more, to return to Grace.

The song is also a clear reference to the Creation of Man. More specifically, in this song, God speaks to Eve.

Of course it is only a symbol, the words can be understood as referring to anyone. Eve is the beginning as the birth and childhood are the beginning for each of us.

"The end is not as fun as the start" shows how the beginning (of life) is both simple and even funny because we are still in innocence and in Grace. The end of life is very different and less funny, not only because it is the end of a cycle, but also and especially because the experiences that we have lived have turned us away from innocence and now we need commitment and repentance to go back to God. Because of this it is recommended to remain a little bit children, to keep within us a bit of that innocence with which we are born.

"I'll give you everything you want/ except the thing that you want" is a reference to the forbidden fruit: God gave to Eve in the Garden of Eden everything she could want except for one thing, which is the temptation to which we also undergo in life. Even God has given us everything except the certainty of a life without sin.

Further in the song seems almost that God Himself should kneel before humanity because He wants more from it. He asks for everything, but not what we are not: we have to account to Him sharing our lives, our choices, our mistakes with Him, and we can not pretend to be what we are not.

Back again the theme of a God who does not abandon the Man: "And you'll never be alone/ come on now show your soul/ you've been keeping your love under control". Man will never be alone because God will always be at his side; God urges him to show his soul, to show it for what it really is, because so far the Man has restricted himself to control the love that is in him without leaving it free to act. Now, with God beside, Love can emanate from every soul and spread.

In the song _"Yahweh"_ there is the spur to continue with confidence to carry messages of love and peace, of course always with God on our side. The song is a prayer, and, as Bono himself said in an interview with the Catholic Avvenire, "The title is an ancient name destined not to be named. I had bypassed it by singing it..... It wants to be a prayer that puts everything in God's hands: from the need for love to the hope that the darkness is defeated".

The song refers to God with the name used in the Old Testament (the title is the name of God as told in Exodus 3 13:14 and already mentioned above for All Because Of You: "I am who I am") even because, as required by the Church, all those who were born (and died) before Christ's death to heal our sins can not ascend to Heaven. We turn then to the eldest God because He could intervene also in favour of all those who can not be with Him only for an "accident" of birth. It is also pointed in the verse "always pain before the child is born?": we ask God the reason of the chaos and of all the pain in this world before the coming of Christ, His Son. The verse can be considered a reference to the expulsion of Eve from Eden ("in sorrow thou shalt give birth").

The song is a pure hymn to God, to His presence and the Love He gives us.

The whole song is a call to God, we want Him to take all of us, both physical and material things, to be able to be with Him, the only thing that is really necessary. "Take this soul/ and make it sing": we offer to God the soul to let it sing. It is locked and dumb in sin, but raising hymns it can return as it was in its origins, in God. "Take this heart/ and make it break" is the culmination of this offering to God: what more than our heart? As Christ offered His heart for humanity, so we offer our mortal heart for eternal life.

The strophe "still waiting for the dawn, the sun is coming up/ the sun is coming up on the ocean/ this love is like a drop in the ocean" describes the Man who is still waiting for rebirth, his own rebirth and that of the world, after the darkness of life. God (the sun) rises from the ocean, from the sea of the corrupt world, and His love is like a drop in the ocean, it's a little thing that almost gets lost in the evil of the world; at the same time it is so great that what it offers us and what we can have in life is only a small part compared to what it will offer us and what we could have once with Him in Heaven.

Further on the Man will ask "why the dark before the dawn" to ask once again to God why so much pain in the world, why before the arrival of Christ only darkness and sin for the Man who awaits the rebirth to be finally in the Light.

In the second strophe the Man asks God to be purified: the hands have to bring the right things and not be fists that can hurt and cause divisions; the mouth should be no cause for criticism and innuendos, but through God's Kiss it must only be the bearer of His message.

In the meantime we finally see the sun rise. From the ocean, from the depths, God comes to us with His Love. Love is like a drop in the ocean, is something that seems to get lost in the immensity that surrounds us, but it is so strong to find and save us.

At the end of the song Man surrenders to God asking Him to take the whole mankind (symbolized by the city) and let it shine with Him, but he also tells Him to do so only if this is what He wants, because the Man can not force God.

"A city should be shining on a hill" is Matthew 5:14: "You are the light of the world. A city built on a hill can not be hid".

"What no man can own, no man can take" is a key verse. If the Man does not know God and His word, if the Man does not follow the right conduct of life, he can not own God, His Grace, eternal life in Heaven. It can also be interpreted as the belonging of Man to God: we have a mortal body which does not belong to us, God has given it to our soul to let the soul make the journey of life. Once in the afterlife, we must abandon our mortal remains, because we are not allowed to take them with us. They belong to God and we are only spirit.

It is also a verse of surrender: we can not take what we can not own; we can not be God, Who is omnipotent.

At the height of the surrender we offer to God our hearts to break because we feel unworthy of Him and of His Love.

In _"Fast cars"_ we must underline a religious reference:

"My garden's overgrown/ I go out on my belly crawling" is an allusion to the serpent of the story of the Fall from Eden and to the curse on the serpent in Genesis 3:14: "Then the Lord God said to the serpent: "Because you have done this, you shall be banned

On your knees

from all the animals and from all the wild creatures; on your belly
shall you crawl, and dirt shall you eat all the days of your life".".

Chapter 13

18 SINGLES (Mercury records, 2006)

The first two collections of the group have been divided in two according to the decades (the first covering the '80s and the second the '90s). This third collection is both more ambitious and more concise, offering a track list of only 18 songs, two of which are new. In just 16 songs, then, the group has set out to retrace and tell the whole story of its musical journey.

Here we analyse the new songs on the album.

"The saints are coming" is a cover of the song by Skyds and is registered together with Green Day.

The song talks about the coming of Christ and of the Saints. The house in New Orleans, bane of many teenagers, symbolizes temptation and sin that creep into life by removing the innocence and letting us join the ranks of sinners.

"Until the clouds unroll and you come down" is found in Revelation 1:7: "Behold, he cometh with clouds; and every eye shall see him, and they also which pierced him: and all kindreds of the heart shall wail because of him. Even so, Amen".

The whole song is littered with references to the coming of Christ. We note among them the following interpretations:

- "I cried to my Daddy on the telephone, how long now": once again we return to the image of the phone call to God, the Father, already used on other occasions by the band. Many Christians refer to prayer as to "the phone of Alleluia".

  God is a good Father, with using the term "daddy" we become familiar with Him and we try to communicate with Him. Again He is asked "how long?" as he had been already asked in songs like <u>Sunday Bloody Sunday</u> and <u>40</u>.

- "How long now till the clouds unroll and you come down" is the coming of Christ. According to the Bible, in fact, the second coming of Christ will take place with a descent from the clouds.

- "But the shadow still remained since your descent": Evil persists after the first coming of Christ on earth and will be completely defeated by His second coming.

- "The saints are coming": on His return to earth Christ will be followed by His heavenly host, the Angels. The Saints are also the souls of the dead who will live in the resurrection of Christ, and then they will come back on earth too.

- "How long now until a weather change condemns belief": it is a reference to the period of tribulation, in which natural events have wiped out all non-believers or those who believed in other religions. How soon will return a similar time, so that only those who believe in Christ will remain?

- "How long now when the nightwatchman lets in the thief" refers to a parable. The "thief" is none other than "the thief in the night" referred to by Jesus himself talking about His return to the earth. When will it be? It has never been established and we can only wait to be saved.

  The figure of the "thief in the night" was already present in the song <u>Seconds</u> of the album War: very directly "like a thief in the night", where it was analysed as a biblical reminder always linked to the new coming of Christ ("for you know very well that the day of the Lordwill come like a thief in the night" (I Thessalonians 5:2))

<u>*"Windows in the sky"*</u> still speaks of resurrection. In the first strophe the concept is expressed very clearly: "The shackles are undone/ the bullet's quit the gun/ the heat that's in the sun/ will keep us when there's none/ The rule has been disproved/ the stone it has been moved/ the grain is now a groove/ all debts are removed". With the return of Christ the chains that kept us anchored to the evil will break, we are again free from sin (to mention a biblical reference we should remember that Paul's letters to the Romans tell us how we were slaves of sin, but the Love of Christ has made us free). The sun's heat is nothing more

than the love of God, ready to support us in the darkest hours, when evil seems to have the upper hand.

Christ rises and breaks every rule in this way: it is normal that after death the body is destined to rot, but this rule is broken by the rising of Christ. The stone of the tomb has been removed, the body is gone and with this certainty we also know that all our debts were paid: Christ took upon Himself all our guilts and all our sins.

"Can't you see what our love has done?" is the amazed finding of what the Love, God, could do: He allowed the resurrection of the Son for the forgiveness of all our sins. Love itself creates enemies for us to test us, but It is ready to intervene and bring back Love. The soul is naked in front of the Love and also hate bends because Love wins on it.

How much God is close to us and our need of Him is described in the strophe "The sky over our head/ we can reach it from our bed/ if you let me in your heart/ and out of my head": we can reach the Heaven without looking for it somewhere. From our bedroom, with our prayers, we can lift our eyes to heaven and attain the Love of God. He must, however, allow us to be in His heart and make us abandon the "head", through Him then we must become pure spirit and leave behind our earthly body.

"Please don't ever let me out of you" is an invocation to God: "Do not let me go, hold me always with You, inside of You". Here returns the fear of abandonment because it is in God that we want to stay and not fall back into sin. The verse "I've got no shame" strengthens the desire: we are not ashamed to turn to God and ask Him to be with Him, but also we are not ashamed to present to Him for what we are, sinners and penitents, hoping and knowing to be able to be with Him.

The key verses are at the very end of the song: "to every broken heart/ for every heart that cries/ love left a window in the skies". Bono emphasizes once again the hope that lies behind the Love of God: God knows that hearts are broken and weep; sin has contaminated them and they mourn their downfall, but Love is so great to always leave a passage to the Heavens for all those who, in faith, want to return to God.

Chapter 14

NO LINE ON THE HORIZON
(Interscope 2009)

The title of the album gives the idea that there is no longer a continuation, no prospects for the future if not the infinite that offers the opportunity to start again (with life, with the struggle, with Love).

In this lack of opportunity is the Christian Faith that can widen the boundaries, pushing the Man beyond the limits to a totally new dimension. We can see that the whole album is an ascent to God through a critical path: the first song is so tied to the last, in which, following the path through all the songs, we find ourselves wondering "You're so high above me, higher than everyone/ Where are you in the Cedars of Lebanon?"

The recordings began in July 2007 in Fez, Morocco.

This choice was dictated by Bono's visit in Morocco at the International Festival of Sacred Music, organized in the city every year.

To record right there and on that occasion has influenced the band in writing the songs of the album.

Indeed, there are strong influences of Hindu and Jewish music and of Sufi singing. Adam himself declares that the music festival was something ancestral.

Unlike the previous albums, many of the texts of <u>No Line on the Horizon</u> are written in the third person; Bono plays the roles of people who have lost their identity and now do not have the time to fight for their values.

There's no boundary line on the horizon, everything is infinite and finite at the same time.

<u>*"No line on the horizon"*</u> speaks of the infinite and there is still a reference to the Holy Spirit which is always a female figure.

"A girl who's like the sea/ I watch her changing everyday for me": the Holy Spirit is like the sea, infinite, and, at the horizon, merged with the sky. In Its many possibilities and forms the Holy Spirit changes and evolves for us to adapt to us in order to be always beside us. The whole universe is contained in the Holy Spirit because it is part of God and God is infinite.

Of particular note are the verses "She said infinity is a great place to start" and "She said "Time is irrelevant, it's not linear"" in which is the Holy Spirit Itself to speak to us of the infinite as a well-known place but without any precise time. The infinite is where it all began, but it is also the place where the past, the present and the future are fused into one same thing and time has no meaning. The infinite is God, the beginning and the end of everything.

Even in this song there is room for a strophe that sings of the loss of Man: "The songs in your head are now on my mind/ you put me on pause/ I'm trying to rewind and replay". The songs that God has taught us are rooted in us, but it is as if we had been paused, in a state of suspension that does not allow us to give voice to these songs. Aware of this we try to "rewind the tape", go back to the time before our lost to resume singing.

The missing dividing line on the horizon can be thus interpreted as a lack of reference that makes us lose, but also as an image of the infinite: as we try to reach the horizon we do not succeed because there is no border on the horizon and it will continue to repeat itself endlessly.

"Magnificent" is an invitation to "magnify" life with Love (here the logical relationship with the prayer to Mary, the Magnificat, but also in a passage of the Confessions of St. Augustine we find a reference to the Magnificat: it says "Magnificently! you could not say anything more divine. This know those who truly love each other").

The Virgin Mary sings Her Joy that comes from having conceived Christ; Her Joy is full of humility, justice and, at the same time, fear.

As a whole, the song is a reference to God as the ultimate form of magnificence, that may be nothing but God.

By analysing the text in particular, we can detect a great number of references to the relationship with God.

At the beginning in the verses "I was born/ I was born to be with you" God is telling us to be born (more precisely embodied in Christ) to be always with us. Specifically, God is with us "in this space and time", now, in our earthly life.

The verses also want to signify how the Man feels bound to the Heavenly Mother even in this earthly life. Perhaps God may seem distant in many moments, but Our Lady is always with us because we are born to be with Her.

"After that and ever after I haven't had a clue/ only to break rhyme/ this foolishness can leave a heart black and blue" describe how after the coming of Christ (and ever since), even if we have tried and try to stay away from God, this is not possible. There is no other way. We can try to break the link (to break the magic of the melody that binds us to God), but only a madness can allow our hearts to remain in darkness. The historical times of the struggle against the Faith had been dark times; dark is the period of our lives when we deny the Faith for sin. Only with hindsight we are back on the right path towards God.

In the verses "Only love, only love can leave such a mark/ only love, only love can heal such a scar" we still speak of love, more particularly of Love, the Love of God. It is the only Love, and the only thing that can make a so deep mark, in life, in history, in Man. And it is the only Love that can heal the scars, that can heal our sins, that can defeat the Evil.

Love leaves signs and sometimes these signs are real scars because Love saves but also knows how to hurt. This same Love is also the only One who can heal the scars as only the Love of a

Mother can do. Even here Love is Salvation, but here more than in any other song Love is the Salvation and the Joy, for it is seen as Motherly Love. Unlike a Father who can also punish a Mother will only forgive without hurting.

"I was born to sing for you/ I didn't have a choice but to lift you up/ and sing whatever song you wanted me to/ I give you back my voice/ from the womb my first cry, it was a joyful noise" strongly express the concept that Man was born to give praise to God, there is no choice, only to raise God with our praises to Him and sing all the songs that He Himself has taught us.

The verses express the devotion to Our Lady: often in their lyrics U2 repeat that God reveals to us His message through songs and He wants us to sing His songs to be near Him and let Him know that we want to be with Him. Here we turn to the Mother by telling Her that it is only for Her that we want to sing, because it is the Mother who comforts and intercedes with a Father who we often feel too impositive and far.

For a mother her son's voice is always joy, even the first cry of the newborn child. Even for the child that crying is joy because it marks the beginning of a life with the Mother.

After the separation from God and the lost in sin, we have to return to Him and sing to Him again our praises. Even before our birth, we sing songs to God and they can only be songs of joy. "It was a joyful noise" is a reference to Psalm 100:1: "Make a joyful noise unto the LORD, all ye lands".

Further on it is emphasized that, with the death of Christ, our sins are forgiven and our whole life long we have to be conscious of this. At the end we will find ourselves with Christ to sing the Glory of the Magnificent, to sing Glory to the Father. "Justified till we die" is nothing but the concept of being forgiven that we find a bit everywhere in the Bible, especially in Paul's Letters. An example is Romans 8:30: "Moreover whom he did predestinate, them he also called: and whom he called, them he also justified: and he whom he justified, them he also glorified".

"You and I will magnify" is instead Luke 1:46-55; it is the song of Mary, also known as the "Magnificat" for its first verse, rendered in the KJV of the Bible as "My soul doth magnify the Lord, and my spirit hath rejoiced in God my Saviour".

The verses "Justified till we die you and I will magnify/ the Magnificent" enclose the concepts of "Justify" and "Magnify". Even though "Magnify" is more often referred to Our Lady here it can be referred to God too: the Virgin Mary leads us to salvation and it is thanks to Her and with Her that we can raise even more The One who is already elevation, God.

At the end of the song, in verse "Only love unites the hearts", we point out that the Love of God not only is with us and pushes us toward Him, but it is also what allows us to live in harmony and peace with all the others. It is only Love that unites hearts and makes us all one, God and Man.

"Moment of surrender" speaks of the solitude in which we live and of the finding of God in it, God Who brings us back to Him.

The song deals with another subject dear to religion: the "surrender" of Man.

The Man bounds himself to release the horses: it comes immediately to my mind the song So Cruel where the horses of love and lust are named. These are the horses that must be let free to run, because free must be our choice between love and sin. It is a field in which we play with fire until we get burned; we are barely conscious that life is a semi-precious stone and it is up to us to turn it into something really valuable or into barren rock. Often we end up making it so dry that even our souls can no longer be part of the "Realm of Certainty". Confusion and doubt get hold us.

In the third strophe we address directly to God, and the conclusion is that the reason of the human uncertainty is not so much the fact that we do not believe in love but rather is that the love does not believe in us and thus we ask God (Love) to believe in us.

"It's not if I believe in love/ But if love believes in me" is an echo of I John 4:10: "This is love: not that we loved God, but that he loved us and sent his Son as an atoning sacrifice for our sins".

There is a moment in which the Man surrenders, submits himself to God, realizing that God is the right way, and at this time of surrender the Man kneels down and sees nothing but the Love around him.

The verses "I've been in every black hole/ at the altar of the dark star/ my body's now a begging bowl/ that's begging to get back" must be quoted: in them we recognize that we had been sinners and want now to go back in the right.

The first part of these verses resume Luke 10:18: "Jesus said, 'I have observed Satan fall like lightning from the sky'.". "Lucifer" is the name that was given to Venus, the morning star; hence the relationship between Satan and the star as the relationship between the dark star and the fall of Satan. The "black hole" is the hell with all its temptations; the "altar of the dark star" symbolizes the worship of the devil (the fallen star that now can no longer shine): having chosen the path of sin we have been followers of Evil. Now we beg for God's Love. We realize the situation and we just want to go back where we were, in that Good that is the rhythm that governs heart, soul and mind, and is not to be controlled.

In the verses "I could see in the reflection/ a face staring back at me" we can read a reference to the Holy Spirit: we look in the mirror and in the reflected image we see someone who looks at us, but it is not our own reflection, it is the Holy Spirit that is in us and reveals Itself. It is a vision beyond the visible that appears to us only when we surrender to God.

In the strophe "I was speeding off the subway/ through the stations of the cross/ every eye looking every other way/ counting down till the pain will stop" we find the reference to the Stations of the Cross. In them we read the meaning of the pain and oppression that Man feels in his existence. Life seems a Way of the Cross, with its obstacles and difficulties. We are surrounded by people, but none seem to notice us, it seems that they ignore us intentionally; we continue to count our stations until the end of our pain and at the end we will find God with us.

In my research I came across a very interesting variant of this strophe, the words "till the pain will stop" are replaced by the words "till the Pentecost" and this variant emphasizes even more what we have just said. It should be analysed in this context the meaning of Pentecost: in the Christian Church Pentecost means the descent of the Holy Spirit that comes as the new law given by God to His believers. For this reason it is also called "The Spirit

Day" and, falling on the fiftieth day after Easter, it ends the Easter period. Pentecost is also the fourteenth (and last) station of "Via Lucis", a liturgical rite in which we remember and celebrate the events of the life of Christ and of the early Church from the resurrection to the Pentecost.

In this, the "via Lucis" is opposed to the "Via Crucis" made of pain and that ends with the deposition of Jesus in the tomb (although in some traditions it will end with a fifteenth station that is the Resurrection of Jesus, creating thus a direct bridge with the "via Lucis", the first station of which is the "Resurrection of Jesus").

In light of these considerations, the strophe can be read as a description of the path that Man follows, from sin to God. Again it is repeated that only the Holy Spirit can save us from sin and bring us back to God.

Unknown caller contains perhaps the words richest of symbols and deeper meanings. The band wants to communicate with the public, but does so in a veiled way, almost hiding the message. And it is in this song that returns the theme of the non-communication, that is a crisis of faith in front of a phone number that has no more an holder.

"3:33 when the numbers fell off the clockface": we can see here the reference to the cover of the album, where it is written "J33: 3" and thus the reference to Jeremiah 33:3: "Call to me and I will answer you and tell you great and unsearchable things you do not know". In an interview with Rolling Stone is reiterated that the number is known to be considered the telephone number of God

Himself.

The invocation to God is right at the beginning: "Sunshine," the Light. Soon after it is said that we are lost in a lonely place, we are lost in darkness ("between the midnight and the dawning"), in the evil, and we invoke the light of God "I was lost" are key words, especially for a Christian, they are the consciousness to be nothing without God.

"Cease to speak that I may speak" can refer to Psalm 46:10: "Be still, and know that I am God; I will be exalted among the nations, I will be exalted in the earth".

We can also see a parallel with the computer language in the verses "Force quit and move to trash/.../ restart and re-boot yourself/ you're free to go//.../ password, you enter here, right now/... // you know your name so punch it in": the" force quit "is, in the Mac language, the forced exit from an out of control program and can not be properly closed. After the extraordinary intervention, the program is removed. So God is able to act on our lives: He can delete them because irrecoverable, "fix them" because no more just, restart them after they have lost themselves. Moreover, we also know the password to enter the system, we just need to enter it: we know what is the right behaviour to go the way of salvation, we know the prayers to God.

The purpose of a prayer to God is not to use His Arm in our favour: He is not a Cosmic Genius. The TRUE meaning of a prayer to God is to allow us to "shut up" in the presence of the Almighty. As Bono sings, the real goal of prayer is to feel God; part of the wonder of prayer is to have the opportunity to stop saying what God can say.

One of the greatest joys of being a Christian is that we may know that we can be faithful in front of the Creator when we pray and it's not because we have been particularly good or saint. Rather, it is because Jesus, the Redeemer, was Good and Holy and Righteous on our behalf, and He shares with us His place standing at the right hand of the Father. We can come in the name of Jesus, instead of Jesus Himself, in front of the Father. We may know that as the Father is favourably disposed toward Jesus, He will be favourable to us too thanks to our relationship with Christ.

The final verse "don't move or say a thing" reminds us for its meaning to Psalm 46:10: "Be still and know that I am God".

Let's see once again how God's presence is strong in us and around us, we just have to stand still and silent, the rest is God and we are aware of this. We must turn to Him and He will guide us on the right path.

After <u>Unknown caller</u> it will be found also in <u>Get on your boots</u> a text that prevails over any other part of the song, a true act of faith, leaving behind the temptations.

<u>"I'll go crazy if I don't go crazy tonight"</u> is a song about finding ourselves back and find Truth. In the first strophe the verse "There's a part of me in the chaos that's quiet" wants to emphasize that even in the extreme confusion that characterizes us there is always a part of us that is stable, that just wants peace.

The verse "how can you stand next to the truth and not see it?" wants to describe the blindness of Man: he is always close to the truth because the truth is in us and around us, yet we can not see or perceive it so great is the confusion in us that ends up to blind us.

The verse "a change of heart comes slow" is a key verse of the song: our hearts will change slowly, slowly we will be able to get out of uncertainty and turn towards the Truth. So, in doubt and in faith, we begin to climb the peaks of sin to reach the Light. In the verse "pity the nation that will not listen to your boys and girls" almost a reference to the biblical passage in which Jesus says "Let the little children come to me", proving that in innocence we will find answers and the possibility of change.

The verses "the sweetest melody is the one we haven't heard/ is it true that perfect love drives out all fear?" renew the claim that what we know is not only what we have to limit ourselves to know, but there is more: it is what we have not and we do not feel that is what we must aspire to. In particular, "Is it true that perfect love drives out all fear" is I John 4:18: "There is no fear in love. But perfect love drives out fear, because fear has to do with punishment. The one who fears is not made perfect in love". It's a rhetorical question, we know that with God and in God every fear disappears to make room for the truth.

"I know I'm not alone" is again the Man who finds he is not alone. Although the road is long and difficult, even if it is a mountain that we must climb and not just a hill, we will face the path "shouting to the darkness, squeeze out sparks of light" because even from the deepest darkness, with God and with faith, we can get the Light.

"Get on your boots" is a song to God in the consciousness that He is with us and we want to turn to Him.

In the second strophe the reference to the night that moves forward and that surrounds us is a reference to Satan, but we are aware that he can not scare us because we know that those ghosts are not real, they are only masks behind which we hide. The only real thing is God.

In the strophe "Here's where we gotta be/ love and community/ laughter is eternity/ if joy is real" the description of Heaven as eternal Joy. We want to be in Communion and Love because if eternal Joy is true this will be our Joy too.

Further on the power of revelation is conferred to the woman: the woman is the symbol of Mary but also the reference to the Holy Spirit which is revelation. In women of the future there is the revelation, thus salvation is yet to come and for now, as sinners, we can only be certain that salvation will come. This certainty is so great that we do not want to hear talk about the wars, almost as if they lose importance in front of the power of God, or if they were a stain on the perfection of our security in God.

At the end of the song God is directly invoked: "God I'm going down/ I don't wanna drown now/ meet me in the sound". There's a melody in the universe, a sound that surrounds us and binds us together. We falter, the crossroad is there again, but we immediately ask God to not let us drown because we do not want to drown; we ask Him to be with us in this surrounding melody because it becomes melody of Love and bring us to Him.

In _"Stand up comedy"_ God is in every strophe. Now we invoke the Love, the world around us is only vertigo, chaos, and the view of Love can disappear, hidden and stolen by someone too in need of

Love. So we feel like we were falling, no longer sustained by Love: "I'm gonna fall down if I can't stand up/ for your love". Not only we fall down, but in falling we abandon Love and can not defend It anymore.

In life we may be born intelligent, but "smart" can also be understood as "elegant." In one word, we are told that we can be born in Good (intelligent to understand what is the right path) or in Evil (elegant because attracted by materialism). We need to fight the beauty as temptress that takes hold of our heart and leads us away from the true beauty that is God.

Here they sing of how the Man is in the image and likeness of God. Faith, Love and Hope give us a boost and help us to risk to be and feel part of the universe.

"I can stand up for hope, faith, love" is found in I Corinthians 13: 13: "And now these three remain: faith, hope and love. But the greatest of these is love" (It is a reference that can also be found in Elvis Ate America). "God is love" again is I John 4:16: "And so we know and rely on the love God has for us. God is love. Whoever lives in love lives in God, and God in him". We can see how many references to John 4 can be found throughout the album!

The verse emphasizes how even in the midst of everything else Hope, Faith and Love are our guides. Nice to note the order in which they are mentioned: first, the Hope that is the hope of being saved, then Faith that is the assurance of salvation, and then Love that is Salvation, all in a spiritual crescendo from sin to God. Now God does not need help anymore to make us understand which is the path, now God is within us and He is the Path.

It's time to stand up and turn to Love.

It's worth quoting the strophe "I gotta stand up to ego but any ego's not really the enemy/ it's like a small child crossing an eight line highway/ on a voyage of discovery": the first thing that comes naturally to do is fight against one own ego, but if we stop to think we are not the enemy. Our ego is nothing but a child, is the innocence that must take risks in its journey of discovery and knowledge from innocence through sin to God.

We have to note the verse "stop helping God across the road like a little old lady" in which the Man is accused of wanting to be a substitute for Christ: God does not need help to carry on His task, we should not be in charged with the responsibility of being the bearers of His message and to renew it. If religion is an "old lady" it must be renewed and God is able to do this, we need only follow His dictates and communicate with Him and with one another to strengthen the Faith and the Love. Again, the God that improves and renews the world can even be thought as science, which develops and makes us evolve.

At the end of the song we find the verses "God is love/ and love is evolution's very best day" which I consider the main verses of the song: we point out the relationship between God and evolution understood as progress and science. Love is the culmination and also the engine of science, so if God is Love, He is both end and means of scientific research and progress. Even science is God and God is in it. Love was born at a specific time but had it been the science or God to create it? Which comes first? In the verse "we're made of stars" it is reaffirmed the scientific concept that in the universe is our origin, we must search the sky and the stars to find out of our world as we know it; at the same time, however, if our origin is in the stars, why do not think of it as origin in God? He is in the Heavens and everything comes from Him. Thus the dichotomy pervades the entire song.

The song is therefore a hymn to the Creator that can be sung even by those who do not believe in God: the Creator, the Love, the first principle is God for believers, science for everyone else.

"White as snow" is the song in which there is Christ, the sacrificial Lamb, that sheds his blood to save the world: "where we can find a lamb as white as snow?". And again we find quotations of John, Revelation, Exodus. Sure, the song is about a land as white as snow, but the only land so pure is the Kingdom of God, and it is easy and obvious the similarity between 'land' and 'lamb'. The title and the subject refer to Isaiah 18: "Come, let us talk this over - says Yahweh - though your sins are like scarlet, they shall be white as snow; though they are red as crimson, they shall be like wool".

The themes of the song are the Love of God and the diversity (whether social, political or religious). It deals with the desire for a new world, more just and acceptable, in which everyone can live in peace and everything is pure. Against the backdrop of these themes we find once again the Psalms, in particular here Psalm 50, with the penitent who begs God to be forgiven for his sins. The sins are washed by the blood of the innocent Lamb, Jesus Christ.

"Who can forgive forgiveness When forgiveness is not only the lamb as white as snow "sing U2," Truly, I was formed in evil, and in sin did my mother give me birth" is what is written in Psalm 51,5. "Who can forgive forgiveness where forgiveness is not/ Only the lamb as white as snow" is also a revival of John 1:29: "The next day John saw Jesus coming toward him and said, 'Look, the Lamb of God, who takes away the sin of the world!'" (we can also see Exodus 12 for a description of the sacrificial lamb of the Passover, which is spotless).

Jesus is the white Lamb that God has sent us and Who is able to forgive all, even when we do not know what forgiveness is.

The Man still lies in its uncertainty, is now in a barren and hostile land, and can only wonder where is now the Lamb of God.

In the last strophe there is the reference to the innocence of childhood: as children we can wander quietly in the forest, we can walk through a treacherous world without fear anything. In adulthood everything changes, the faces that we meet are all "wolves", all enemies and tempters.

And yet at the end of the song there is a bitter observation: "If only a heart could be as white as snow" echoes Psalm 51.7: "Make me free from sin with hyssop: let me be washed whiter than snow". If only it were possible to maintain innocence, if only the heart remained white as snow, if only we could be like Jesus.

We can read the song as the journey of Man: at the beginning everything is easy, the age of childhood is only play games and lightheartedness, then we know God and with Him the world, which contrasts Him with sin. We feel the need to go back to innocence and the only way is through a pure heart, the heart of Christ.

**"Breathe"** sings of the desire to go on living, to be out of the confusion and find Grace.

"Everyday I die again, and again I'm reborn" highlights the mechanical cyclic nature of Man's life: every day we wake up, we are reborn to life; each day we die having spent the day in a world of sinners and temptations to be reborn again the next day.

We need to find the courage to go out every day in the street and deal with life. "I got a love you can't defeat" emphasizes the consciousness that Man is not alone: by his side there is a Love so big and strong that It can not be defeated; next to him is God.

The verses "the roar that lies on the other side of silence/ the forest fire that is fear so deny it" propose the contrast Good/ Evil present in Man. The silence is, paradoxically, the state of confusion related to Man. On the one hand a roar that shakes, on the other hand the forest that burns: Good calls, the Evil scars but it is there and cannot be denied.

Finally we can breathe conscious of having rejected the sin, and here comes back again the theme of the music as a means to meet God and find our way. The songs are in us and should be worn as a crown: the hymns we sing elevate us to God.

"I found grace inside a sound/ I found grace, it's all that I found". It is in the songs, in their melody, that we can find Grace. It's the only thing we find because in front of Grace everything disappears, there is no longer the world, there is no more evil. In Grace we breathe, free from everything and close to God.

"Cedars of Lebanon"

All throughout the Bible there are references to the "Cedars of Lebanon". We can cite for example the Song of Songs 5:15: "His legs are pillars of marble set on bases of pure gold. His appearance is like Lebanon, choice as its cedars".

In this regard, we can also cite Psalms 29:5 "The voice of God breaks the cedars; the LORD breaks in pieces the cedars of Lebanon".

Why the cedars of Lebanon? Tradition has it that these are giant plants that can grow up to 40 meters (again the reference to the number forty, as we have already analysed in the song 40) and have a trunk circumference of 10 meters. The voice that can break them must be really an infinitely powerful voice. It can only be the voice of God.

"I am here 'cause I don't wanna go home" is not wanting to go back home, here intended as the house of God, to be back to our origins, because too big is the shame for our sins, the guilt for our sins. The sense of exile from one own house is the foundation of the doctrine of the Fall and of original sin: it is after the fall and original sin that we can not feel at home in a world so steeped in sin, but this helps us to find what is the right way home to God.

If at the beginning of the album we could find a song that left a glimpse of the possibility of an optimistic call for the transcendent presence of God in the world, here, as in a full circle, we find expressed the desire for an effective presence and tangible expression of God in the world "(you are) so high above me, higher than everyone/ where are you in the cedars of Lebanon?" is the consciousness of the distance from God, lifted up on us, Guide and Reference, but also detached and unattainable Observer.

The whole song contains many verses that may be referred to the Song of Solomon: we can see reference to the story of husband and wife separated but intent to meet to be together again. Among all, let's consider the verses "this shitty world sometimes produces a rose/ the scent of it lingers and then it just goes/ where are you in the cedars of Lebanon?" which refer to "the beams of our house are cedar, our rafters are pine/ I am a rose of Sharon, a lily of the valleys.../ his appearance is like Lebanon, choice as the cedars", which is part of the Song of Solomon.

Of course here the relationship that is lost and must be rediscovered is not between husband and wife, but between Man and God.

Chapter 15

B-SIDES AND MISCELLANEOUS TRACKS

"A celebration" is a song released as a single that does not belonging to any album in March 1982, in the year between the outputs of <u>Boy</u> ('81) and <u>War</u> ('83). The song was later re-released on two occasions, namely in the collection The Complete U2 in 2004 and in the bonus disc of the remastered version of October in 2008.

The main theme of the song is a celebration of what we believe in and in particular the right to be free, politically free but also religiously free.

"I believe you can loose these chains" can refer to God as well as to the Holy Spirit. Both can loosen the chains that keep us from being free and force us to remain in the material world, in sin. I would be more inclined to opt for a reference to the Holy Spirit by considering the following verse: it is not God whom we ask to dance with us, but rather to the Holy Spirit that we want always with us in our journey of life. Nothing can take the upper hand on us if It will be next to us.

The double meaning, religious and political, is clearly visible in the verses "I believe in the bells of Christchurch/ ringing for this land/ I believe in the cells of Mountjoy/ there's an honest man": Christchurch is the oldest cathedral in Dublin and seat of the Anglican archbishop. It is however officially recognized as the seat of the bishop of the Roman Catholic Church (who physically stays at St. Mary's). The belief in the sound of these bells is the belief in the possibility of peaceful coexistence between the two different doctrines, as it is the belief in the possibility of a united Ireland and an Ireland in peace.

The reference to Mountjoy is more closely related to politics, since it is the name of the prison located in Phibsbow in the centre of Dublin which has the largest population of prisoners in Ireland and in which Thomas Ashe died after a hunger strike. He was then taken as an example for many of the protests of the IRA. At Mountjoy were taken into custody the prisoners condemned to deportation before being deported to Van Diemen's Land (the name that Europeans used to Tasmania, part of the Irish West Indies). We recall here that Van Diemen's Land is a song dedicated to the poet John Boyle O'Reilly, who had been deported and, after fleeing to America, become spokesman for the Irish community and its culture.

"I believe in the walls of Jericho/ I believe they're coming down" is a reference to the Gospel of Jesus, 6: 1-5: "Now the gates of Jericho were securely barred because of the Israelites. No one went off and no one came in. Then the Lord said to Joshua, "See, I have delivered Jericho into your hands, along with its king and its fighting men. March around the city once with all the armed men, do this for six days. Have seven priests carry trumpets of ram's horn in front of the ark. On the seventh day, march around the city seven times, with the priests blowing the trumpets. When you hear them sound a long blast on the trumpets, have the whole army give a loud shout; then the wall of the city will collapse and the army will go up, everyone straight in".". We can also notice a reference to Joshua 6:20: "When the trumpets sounded, the people shouted, and at the sound of the trumpets, when the people gave a loud shout, the wall collapsed; so every man charged straight in, and they took the city". The reference to the sound of trumpets connects to the following verses in which returns also the reference to the children because it is with their innocence that we can still hope for Salvation. The "city kids" are also the Angels of Heaven.

"Alex descends into hell for a bottle of milk/ korova 1"
"Dies irae, dies illa/ Dies irae, dies illa Tuba mirum spargens sonum" refers to the Mass Requiem: "Dies irae/ dies illa/ Tuba mirum/ Spargens sonum (In the day of wrath/ That day/ The trumpet's wondrous call/ Sounding abroad)" and also to 1 Corinthians 15:52: "... in an instant, in the blink of an eye, at the last trumpet. For the trumpet will sound, the dead will be raised incorruptible, and we shall be changed". We notice how the last verse "Descendit in Inferno "is not part of the Dies Irae but is taken from the Creed: "He descended into Hell").

The song *"Salome"* (February 1992), as well as Oscar Wilde's <u>Salome</u>, picks up the story of the death of John the Baptist. Therefore let's see Mark 6:17-29: "Give you half what I got if you untie the knot, it's a promise" and Mark 6:22-23: "Herodias' own daughter came in and performed a dance that delighted Herod and his guests. The king said to the girl, 'Ask of me whatever you wish and I will grant it to you'. He even swore [many things] to her, 'I will grant you whatever you ask of me, even to half of my kingdom'".

"Baby I feel sick, do not make me stick to a promise" is from Mark 6:25-26: "The girl hurried back to the king's presence and made her request, 'I want you to give me at once on a platter the head of John the Baptist'. The king was deeply distressed, but because of his oaths and the guests he did not wish to break his word to her".

"Falling at your feet" is part of the <u>Million Dollar Hotel</u>'s soundtrack.

The song emphasizes the complete submission to God and to His will.

"Every knee not ready to bend" can be seen in Philippians 2:9-10: "...God greatly exalted him and bestowed on him the name that is above every name, that at the name of Jesus every knee should bend, of those in heaven and on earth and under the earth". The long list of everything that falls at the feet of God proceeds until the last verses in which we address directly to God, once again lost in uncertainty. To Him we ask who we must believe in, to Him we ask to teach us to surrender (still appears the word "surrender" so dear to the religion). The last verse is the key verse of the song and almost sums up the meaning of the message that U2 wants to convey. "Not my will, THY will", it's not my will but Thy Will, with Thy deliberately written in all capital letters to indicate that it is really God's Will. The verse can be found in Matthew 26:39: Jesus' prayer in the Garden of Gethsemane: "He advanced a little and fell prostrate in prayer, saying, 'My Father, if it is possible, let this cup pass from me; yet, not as I will, but as you will'.".

<u>Always</u> is a real prayer in which we give ourselves to God and we want God.

"Here today, gone tomorrow" is the fleeting nature of time: today we are here, tomorrow we will be no more. Life is short and maybe there is not so much time to walk the road to God. We must always keep what we have and convince us that everything that we lost was not really necessary.

"Put your head over the parapet" is Matthew 4:5-6: the temptation of Jesus: "Then the devil took him to the holy city, and made him stand on the parapet of the temple, and said to him, 'If you are the Son of God, throw yourself down. For it is written: 'He will command his angels concerning you' and "with their hands they will support you, lest you dash your foot against a stone"'".

"Get down off your holy cloud, always/ God will not deal with the proud, always/ well if you dream then dream out loud, always/ eternally yours, always" are verses that tell us to be modest because God is not with those that are superior, but only with the weakest, the smallest, the most insignificant. The verses urge to let our thoughts and fantasies free because it is only "dreaming out loud" that we can establish a contact with God and with each other too. The verse "eternally yours" is to give oneself to God for eternity. The following verses emphasize the devotion by repeating "I want you": we are urged to look for ourselves in the other (we are all brothers in God) and we ask God to wait for us because sooner or later we will come to Him, in the meantime we have to share that moment that unites us all that is the moment when words become prayer. The concluding lines "now and forever/ for always" have a sense of "amen" at the conclusion of our conversation with God, because it will be forever so.

"Levitate" is a song dedicated to the Holy Spirit. It is in the Spirit that we can find the message and have peace. "Spirit come on down/ No, I'm not coming down" are repeated several times, asking the Holy Spirit to descend upon us because we do not want to get off, do not want to leave the state of grace to sink into the sin. We want to get the most hidden secrets of Love and nothing can stop us now because we know we want all the Love and It must be as hard as hate to be able to win on it. Only with the Holy Spirit, and with Love, we can enjoy freedom because it is thanks to Them that we are able to free ourselves from all that is earthly and is evil. References to the Holy Spirit descending from Heaven can be found in many passages in the Bible, for example in Luke 3:21-22 ("Now it came about that when all the people had been given baptism, Jesus, having had baptism with them, was in prayer, when, the heaven being open, The Holy Spirit came down in the form of a dove, and a voice came from heaven, saying, You are my dearly loved Son, with whom I am well pleased" and Acts 2:1-4 (And when the day of Pentecost was come, they were all together in one place. And suddenly there came from heaven a sound like the rushing of a violent wind, and all the house where they were was full of it. And they saw tongues, like flames of fire, coming to rest on every one of them. And they were all full of the Holy Spirit, and were talking in different languages, as the Spirit gave them power).

"Through the locked doors" is in John 20:19: "On the evening of that first day of the week, when the disciples were together, with the doors locked for fear of the Jews, Jesus came and stood among them and said, 'Peace be with you!'".

"Who can stop us now/ who could make us wait/ who could slow us down" underline the strength with which we desire Love. We caught a glimpse of the way and with the help of the Holy Spirit we started to follow it. Now nothing and no one can hinder us in any way.

The song ends with another invocation to the Holy Spirit because it is only through It that we can come to God.

"Mercy" is a song that Bono sings to God for the Love he has for Christ. The theme of Jesus is a leitmotif for the majority of the verses: for "I was drinking some wine and it turned to blood" we can cite, among others, 1 Corinthians 11:23-25: "For I received from the Lord what I also passed on to you: The Lord Jesus, on the night he was betrayed, took bread, and when he had given thanks, he broke it and said, 'This is my body, which is for you, do this in remembrance of me'. In the same way, after supper he took the cup, saying, 'This cup is the new covenant in my blood; do this, whenever you drink it, in remembrance of me'.". The wine that becomes blood, the Last Supper and the communion in Christ; we are one with Him.

In the second verse, almost in contrast with the sense of spirituality that is steeped in the first, we talk of religion: religion is only meaningful if we are among the good, for the others it makes no sense because it does not exist or because religion wants only reward the deserving. There is a marked difference between religion and Faith, between True Love and religion.

There follows a series of combinations that want to emphasize how much we are "ONE" with God:

- "With your telescope... I can see further": it is through God's eyes that we can see far.

- "We're a binary code... a one and a zero": as in a binary code ones and zeros are inseparably united, so God and Man depend on each other. If there is no God there is no Man, but without Man there can not be a God.

- "You are gravity... searching for the ground": gravity, to be such, must exercise its power on land and so God needs a confirmation to send out Love.

- "You are silence... searching for a sound": God is silence, pure thought, but the thought has to find a voice to spread his message.

- "Your heart is aching... your heart is my home": the Heart of God is our home even if it is a Heart that suffers. It suffers because Man tends to move away but suffers because, in the figure of Christ, was pierced and broken.

- "It's fascinating... I know I'll never be alone" is a clear statement that the union with God is eternal, that He will never leave us alone.

Of particular note are the verses "Love will come again/ I'll be gone again" that are repeated also in the variant "Love has come again/ I am gone again": in the first case the certainty that Love will come back to save us, in the the second case the finding that Love has already arrived and we are already saved.

We become insensitive to the power of Love because It fills us so completely to leave no room for anything else, not even to the emotions.

At the end of the song stands out the verse "Love is the end of history" which brings us back to the theme of God as the ultimate goal of life: we are born in God, we live in sin, we will die in God to live in His Love for eternity.

Further on "Love has come again" is repeated, this time followed by the verse "I'm alive again" that leads the way to the apex of the song: with the coming of Love we can reborn. It is an inner rebirth because, coming from the state of sinners, we can reborn in God, but it is also a spiritual rebirth because after the Day of Judgement we will all be in the Grace of God for eternity.

The final verses connect to this sense of rebirth in God; they are sung to fade into a sense of infinity: "I'm alive, I'm born again and again and again..." which clearly takes John 3:3: "In reply Jesus declared, 'I tell you the truth, no one can see the kingdom of God unless he is born again'.".

Finally, we can say to be alive because at the end of our journey there is God and in His Love we are resurrected.

"Waves of sorrow (Birdland)" can be read almost like a prayer.

The mist that rises from the hill of hell is the doubt and the temptation that beset Man. In the verses "You walk through the night/ to get here today" we see the fight of Man against sin and evil in order to be in Good and in God.

Now the sun is a cruel sun because it is not Light but a sun that radiates cruelty, we feel sick although not in the evil.

"And if the rain come... now/ would it wash us all away": a purifying rain is invoked. We can instinctively compare this with the Great Flood narrated in the Bible: as the flood swept away a humanity that lived only to sin, so now the rain has to wash away our sins and make us pure.

We wonder where the holy cities and the ancient sacred scrolls are; everything that was precious now is no more. In return we expect more, even more valuable things. I emphasize here a biblical reference: "Where now the Emperor Menelik/ and the Queen of Sheba's gold": the visit of the Queen of Sheba to King Solomon is reported in 1 Book of Kings 10. The Ethiopian tradition has it that the Ethiopian Emperor Menelik was the son of the Queen of Sheba and King Solomon.

Christ is invoked ("Oh son of the shepherd boy now king/ What wisdom can you bring" which is a clear biblical reference: the King David is the shepherd, his son is King Solomon; the story of how Solomon got his immense knowledge is found in the Book of Kings 1, 3) and He is asked what wisdom can bring and what songs can sing. He is asked where the music of angels is, and in particular the music of the Seraphim (angels that belong, together with Cherubim and Thrones, to the first hierarchy of angels, the highest angelic order, the closer to God. In the Bible it is said that they sing the music of the spheres, regulating the movement of the heavens as They have been commanded, and burning with Love and zeal for God give off a light so bright and powerful that none but the divine eyes can look at Them).

A series of categories that are worthy of blessing follows. It is recognized in this list the reference to the Gospel that defines

blessed all the more vulnerable and marginalized: "Blessed are the meek who scratch in the dirt/ For they shall inherit what's left of the earth" echoes the words of bliss, as in Matthew 5:3-10 (a quote saying: "Blessed are the meek, for they will inherit the earth").
"They are buried in this valley of dry bones" refers to Ezekiel's vision as in Ezekiel 37:1-3: "The hand of the LORD was upon me, and he brought me out by the Spirit of the LORD and set me in the middle of a valley; it was full of bones. He led me back and forth among them, and I saw a great many bones on the floor of the valley, bones that were very dry. He asked me, "Son of man, can these bones live?" I said, "O Sovereign LORD, you alone know".
Especially with the last verse, the Holy Spirit that is able to defeat all is blessed. It is the Spirit of God Who is always winning, but also, due to the sense of the previous verses, the spirit of those who are able to defeat sin and evil and return to God.

**"Hold me, thrill me, kiss me, kill me"** is a song full of references to Christ and to Love. In the title the combination of "kiss me" and "kill me" reminds us to Judas' betrayal and to the death of Jesus. The entire title, then, is a description of Love: what else can, at the same time, hold (almost tight in a hug), thrill, kiss and kill?
The song describes the human condition and the continuous search for God.
The repetition of the line "you're a star" underlines the importance it has for the Man to be at the centre of attention, to be greater than the others, like a star in the sky, like God.
The world turns in the wrong direction, we steal those that have

already stolen, honesty does not exist, be a prostitute is considered an art, it does not matter how you get things but just to have them. The verses "oh no, don't be shy/ you don't have to go blind" urged the Man not to be shy, not to be ashamed if he wants to find good in evil, not to become blind but to continue to see the good in the evil that surrounds him. The chorus sounds like a Q & A with God where God calls the Man and the Man simply says, "hold me, thrill me, kiss me, kill me" as if invoking God on his side.

In the third strophe it returns the theme of the doubt: "You don't know how you got here/ you just know you want out" describe a Man that becomes conscious of being in the wrong place. Now it does not matter to know how we have arrived there, it is important to know we want to leave. We are once again at the crossroad of life: we are in evil and we want to be back in the good. The two paths diverge and as always, the choice is not so obvious and simple. The doubt is there and is well expressed in the two following verses: "believing in yourself/ almost as much as you doubt". The Man believes in his abilities, but doubt that assails him is as strong as his confidence.

The refrain is now repeated in the variant "it takes a crowd to cry" that brings to my mind the crowd mourning the death of Christ. Linked to the previous verse I interpret it as referring to a Man who isolates himself, that is ashamed of what he is, but is urged not to be ashamed and to join with others in prayer and repentance to feel finally free and pure, ready for God.

The last strophe contains a direct reference to Jesus. We expect the best from every man, we want him to live a perfect life as that of Jesus, but no one can be Jesus. "They'll want their money back/ if you're alive at thirty-three" refers to the death of Christ. He died at thirty-three years, so if we will still be alive at that age will mean that we are not like Him. The reference to money that have to be back makes me think on one hand to the betrayal of Judas (if Jesus is not killed the thirty pieces of silver must be returned), on the other hand it may be also a bet on Man: if the Man will not be able to live like Jesus the bet is lost. The only thing in common between Jesus and the Man is the crucifix: as Jesus took it on Calvary so everyone has his own cross to bear for life.

The last chorus is presented as a direct reference to Love and God: "of course you're not shy/ you don't have to deny love". Finally, the Man comes out of his isolation conscious of not being alone because God is with him, he just has to find the courage not to deny Love because Love is in him and is the ultimate goal of life.

Electrical Storm talks definitely of sensual and erotic love and this is also clear from the video of the song.

Reading between the lines we can easily interpret some verses according to spiritual love.

"The sea it swells like a sore head/ and the night it is aching" describe the rebellious nature that hurts and the painful night: Evil invades the world upsetting nature and taking away that inner peace that was characteristic of being in God.

The entire second strophe can be read as referring to God: God is the thought that constantly occupies the mind of Man, but it is still not enough. Even the sky can crack (it is the Day of Judgement), but whatever thing may happen there is always hope because there is always a way to get back, one way to get out of the state of sinners to return to Love and only in Love. Only with Love this is possible.

The verses "Let's see colors that have never be seen/ let's go to places no one else has been" are very significant. The verses are the willing to break away from the world to go towards God. Heaven is a new place where no one has gone before, it is the place where there are new colours, colours that have never be seen because they are the colours of Good and Grace.

The "electrical storm" is that spark of universal energy that is released when good and evil collide. We feel that it burns like hell, we hope that the storm breaks soon and we hope in the rain, the water that purifies, to wash away sin and allow us to be back in God, away from evil.

Chapter 16

CONCLUSION

We can therefore conclude that in the music of U2 there are really religion, spirituality and faith; the desire to convey a message that will endure in everyone's life. This is at least what I set out to read in their songs through this book.

It is true also that there are many other interpretations and messages in their songs. Here I've chosen the faith, and, as an atheist convinced, I found really a lot of it in their songs.

The Osservatore Romano published on 4-5 January 2010, speaking of U2 and belief, contains interesting observations on the matter. It reports a comment by Bono, in which he says: "In the music of U2 there are cathedrals and streets. The streets lead to the cathedrals, and as you walk on them you feel nervous, as if someone were following you. If you turn around there is no one. Then finally you enter in cathedrals and only then you realize that there really is someone following you: God".

On the same Osservatore we find an interesting comment by Morandi. According to him, the work of U2 proposes itself as a circular path: from the intimity and the religiosity of the early records, we go through the loss of Zooropa in which Bono "surrenders and confesses to have lost compass and maps, reasons and religion, limits and boundaries", and which contains The first time, a song in which, starting from the parable of the prodigal son, reflects on the loss of faith. And it also goes through Pop, a disc "full of discussions with God", in search of the lost road. We get up to <u>No Line On The Horizon</u>, the twelfth and last album of the group, where they found the light and the hope of the beginning, particularly in <u>Magnificent</u>, a praise to God, a "final hymn to love", and in <u>Unknown caller</u>, where the unknown who calls us is the God who saves.

But - adds Morandi - "the thing that makes the lyrics of Bono compelling is the sincerity with which he puts forward a faith made up of questions addressed to a God who is near, a friend with whom one can even quarrel".

I would like to conclude by quoting what Bruce Springsteen said about U2 into the Rock & Roll House of Fame (2005): "In their music you feel the spirituality... how you do find God unless He is not in your heart... I think this is a big part of what has kept the band together all these years. See, the bands form by accident, but it is not by chance that they survive".

BIBLIOGRAPHY

Andrea Morandi, <u>U2. The name of love</u>, Arcana,Roma 2009

Art Rock XIV, <u>U2 testi originali con traduzione a fronte</u>, Edizioni Grafiche Lo Vecchio

Irvine McKenzie, <u>Parola di Bono Vox</u>, Aliberti Editore, Roma, 2008

Loris Cantarelli, <u>U2 1979-2004: 25 anni di inquietudine rock</u>, Editori Riuniti, Roma, edizione 2005

From internet:

<u>www.angolotesti.it</u>

<u>www.atU2.com</u>

<u>www.songmeanings.com</u>

<u>La Bibbia – Bilingue | Italiano-Inglese |</u>, <u>www.transcripture.com</u>

<u>www.u2.com</u>

<u>www.wikipedia.org</u>

Finito di stampare
nel mese di aprile 2025
presso Rotomail Italia S.p.A. – Vignate (MI)